PASSING THE GEORGIA 8TH GRADE CRCT

IN

English / Language Arts

(2006)

Devin Pintozzi

American Book Company
PO Box 2638
Woodstock, GA 30188-1383
Toll Free: 1 (888) 264-5877   Phone: (770) 928-2834
Toll Free Fax: 1 (866) 827-3240
Web site: www.americanbookcompany.com

ACKNOWLEDGEMENTS

The authors would like to acknowledge the technical and editing assistance of Marsha Torrens.

All the characters, places, and events portrayed in this book are fictitious, and any resemblance to real people, places, or events is purely coincidental.

This product/publication includes images from CorelDRAW 9 and 11 which are protected by the copyright laws of the United States, Canada, and elsewhere. Used under license.

Georgia 8th Grade CRCT ELA
Table of Contents

Chapter 4   Sentences/Subject-Verb Agreement   75

Chapter 5   Adjectives, Adverbs, Using Negative Words   93

Chapter 6   Sentence Errors and Sequencing   105

Chapter 7   Spelling   119

Chapter 8   Paragraphs   135

PREFACE

Passing the Georgia 8th Grade CRCT in English/Language Arts will help students who are learning or reviewing material for the CRCT. The materials in this book are based on the testing standards as published by the Georgia Department of Education.

This book contains several sections. These sections are as follows: 1) General information about the book; 2) A Diagnostic Test; 3) An Evaluation Chart; 4) Chapters that teach the concepts and skills that improve graduation readiness; 5) Two Practice Tests. Answers to the tests and exercises are in a separate manual. The answer manual also contains a Chart of Standards for teachers to make a more precise diagnosis of student needs and assignments.

We welcome comments and suggestions about the book. Please contact the author at

American Book Company
PO Box 2638
Woodstock, GA 30188-1383

Toll Free: 1 (888) 264-5877
Phone: (770) 928-2834
Fax: (770) 928-7483
Web site: www.americanbookcompany.com

ABOUT THE AUTHOR

Devin Pintozzi earned a BA from Oglethorpe University in Atlanta, Georgia. In 2003, he was awarded an MBA from Georgia State University. He is the author of several best-selling books in language arts and social studies. Clear and concise communication of the written word is his goal.

TEST-TAKING TIPS

1 Complete the chapters and practice tests in this book. This text will help you review the skills for English/Language Arts: Reading. The book also contains materials for reviewing skills under the Research standards.

2 Be prepared. Get a good night's sleep the day before your exam. Eat a well-balanced meal, one that contains plenty of proteins and carbohydrates, prior to your exam.

3 Arrive early. Allow yourself at least 15–20 minutes to find your room and get settled. Then you can relax before the exam, so you won't feel rushed.

4 Think success. Keep your thoughts positive. Turn negative thoughts into positive ones. Tell yourself you will do well on the exam.

5 Practice relaxation techniques. Some students become overly worried about exams. Before or during the test, they may perspire heavily, experience an upset stomach, or have shortness of breath. If you feel any of these symptoms, talk to a close friend or see a counselor. They will suggest ways to deal with test anxiety. **Here are some quick ways to relieve test anxiety:**

- Imagine yourself in your most favorite place. Let yourself sit there and relax.
- Do a body scan. Tense and relax each part of your body starting with your toes and ending with your forehead.
- Use the 3-12-6 method of relaxation when you feel stress. Inhale slowly for 3 seconds. Hold your breath for 12 seconds, and then exhale slowly for 6 seconds.

6 Read directions carefully. If you don't understand them, ask the proctor for further explanation before the exam starts.

7 Use your best approach for answering the questions. Some test-takers like to skim the questions and answers before reading the problem or passage. Others prefer to work the problem or read the passage before looking at the answers. Decide which approach works best for you.

8 Answer each question on the exam. Unless you are instructed not to, make sure you answer every question. If you are not sure of an answer, take an educated guess. Eliminate choices that are definitely wrong, and then choose from the remaining answers.

9 Use your answer sheet correctly. Make sure the number on your question matches the number on your answer sheet. In this way, you will record your answers correctly. If you need to change your answer, erase it completely. Smudges or stray marks may affect the grading of your exams, particularly if they are scored by a computer. If your answers are on a computerized grading sheet, make sure the answers are dark. The computerized scanner may skip over answers that are too light.

10 Check your answers. Review your exam to make sure you have chosen the best responses. Change answers only if you are sure they are wrong.

Georgia 8th Grade English/Language Arts Diagnostic Test

NOTE: All standards referenced are English Language Arts

1. What is the structure of the sentence below?   8C1b

> The horses galloped; the riders spurred them on.

   A. compound   C. compound-complex

   B. complex   D. simple

2. The sentence below contains a dangling modifier. Select the sentence that is rewritten correctly.   8C1c

> After a few years of playing music, medicine became his choice of study.

   A. Medicine became his chosen course of study after a few years of playing music.

   B. While playing music, medicine became his chosen course of study.

   C. After he played music for a few years, medicine became his chosen course of study.

   D. He played music a few years after medicine became his chosen course of study.

3. Which sentence in the paragraph below is unrelated to the main idea?   8W2

> **1.** After the Civil War, many blacks moved to the West to find a better life for themselves. **2.** Some became cowhands, ranchers, or shopkeepers **3.** Most people had to travel great distances to get to a general store. **4.** Some farmed the land in a harsh environment with few resources. **5.** Several African-American Army regiments served on the frontier and became skilled fighters.

   A. 1   B. 2   C. 3   D. 4

4. **How should the punctuation be corrected in the sentence below?** 8C1g

> Silly Boy, the teachers pet, didn't stay in class very long.

   A. Remove the comma after *pet*.

   B. Add an apostrophe between the *r* and *s* in *teachers*.

   C. Remove the comma after *Boy*.

   D. Add a comma after *class*.

5. **Which sentence below is a compound sentence?** 8C1b

   A. My sister has 4 children and works at the mall.

   B. The Braves lost the first three games, but they won the series.

   C. My friend was born in Canada but later moved to the United States.

   D. My favorite dinner is a hamburger, French fries, and a chocolate shake.

6. **Which word BEST fits in the blank in the sentence below?** 8C1a

> Amanda delivered the Chihuahua to _____ new owner.

   A. their   C. it's

   B. its   D. you're

Read the following paragraph and answer the question which follows.

> However, when the eagle heard what a warm-hearted little fellow the tortoise was, he went to pay a call on him. The tortoise family showed such pleasure in his company and fed him so lavishly that the eagle returned again and again, while every time as he flew away he laughed, "Ha, ha! I can enjoy the hospitality of the tortoise on the ground, but he can never reach my nest in the tree-top!"

7. **Which of the following sentences should be placed at the beginning of the paragraph?**

   A. It was not often that the tortoise and the eagle met, for the one spent his days in the clouds and the other under a bush.

   B. The eagle did as the tortoise suggested.

   C. The eagle flew away with the food.

   D. The eagle flew high into the clouds and darted down with the speed of an arrow. 8W1

8. **Choose the sentence in which the apostrophe is used correctly.** 8C1g

   A. Dakota and Caroline's home is in the mountains.

   B. We watered our neighbors plants' while they were on vacation.

   C. The runners-ups' names were announced before Miss America's name.

   D. The girl's lockers are in the gym.

9. **How would the sentence below change if *bear* were changed to *bears*?** 8C1a

> The bear eats honey every chance he gets.

   A. The bears eat honey every chance he gets.

   B. The bears eats honey every chance they gets

   C. The bears eat honey every chance they get.

   D. The bears eats honey every chance they get.

10. **Which of the following sentences is punctuated correctly?** 8C1g

   A. "After all that work," Jake asked, "why did you just give up"?

   B. "After all that work, Jake asked, why did you just give up?"

   C. "After all that work", Jake asked, "why did you just give up"?

   D. "After all that work," Jake asked, "why did you just give up?"

11. **In which of the following sentences is the case of the pronouns correct?** 8C1a

   A. She and I went to the game together.

   B. We saw her and him together at the game.

   C. Dave asked Jim and he to help put back the chairs.

   D. We and them will be going to high school next year.

12. **Which of the following is a complete sentence?** 8C1b

   A. He walked aimlessly.

   B. Mike saw the headlights they were very bright.

   C. The mice ran the cats chased them.

   D. Looking for my keys but I couldn't find them.

13. **List the number of each sentence in the logical order that would make a good paragraph.** 8W1

   1. Do not leave the waiting room until your name is called.

   2. Make an appointment over the phone to see a doctor.

   3. Pay for services rendered.

   4. Sign in at the reception desk at the time of your appointment.

   A. 3-2-1-4   C. 1-4-2-3

   B. 1-2-3-4   D. 2-4-1-3

14. **Which of the following is a fragment?**

   A. She rode in the car. 8C1b

   B. At the end of the street.

   C. Greg went home.

   D. Birds have feathers.

15. **Erica got up and ran after _____ and _____.** 8C1a

   A. she   him

   B. him   she

   C. he   she

   D. him   her

16. **Which of these two brands of paint covers _____?** 8C1f

   A. more complete

   B. completely

   C. more completely

   D. most completely

17. **I have _____ this scene before.** 8C1d

   A. drawed   C. drawn

   B. drew   D. draw

18. **Read the sentence below. Then identify the underlined part of the sentence.** 8C1f

   When the dance was over, <u>Derek walked me home</u>

   A. phrase

   B. independent clause

   C. dependent clause

   D. prepositional phrase

19. Which sentence below is written correctly? 8C1e

A. Although my dad is old enough to retire, he decided to work for another year.

B. Although my dad is old enough to retire; he decided to work for another year.

C. Although my dad is old enough to retire. He decided to work for another year.

D. Although my dad is old enough to retire, he decided to work for another year

20. In the sentence below, what changes should be made to correct the capitalization errors? 8C1g

> Although I was born in the south, I don't have a southern accent because my parents are from New York city.

A. Use a capital *S* in *south* and a capital *S* in *southern*.

B. Use a capital *S* in *southern* and a capital *C* in *city*.

C. Use a capital *S* in *south* and a capital *C* in *city*.

D. Use a capital *S* in *south* and a small letter *y* in *York*.

21. Which of the following sentences contains a misplaced modifier? 8C1c

A. Last night I watched a television show about earthquakes.

B. Bryan served strawberry shortcake to his friends covered in whipped cream.

C. Jessica told me she would call you sometime tomorrow.

D. Mary needs to read three more books before the end of the semester.

22. Which sentence below has a prepositional phrase underlined correctly? 8C1f

A. <u>How many stars</u> are in the universe?

B. All of the boats are <u>sailing for the island</u>.

C. Professor Kline combined the elements <u>in a beaker</u>.

D. The five tigers have been eating <u>more than usual</u>.

Choose the correct word or words to complete each sentence for questions 23 – 25.

23. The hurricane made the rain come down like pellets beating us _____. 8C1f

A. ferocious   C. ferociously

B. fierceness   D. hardly

24. Eileen _____hands her homework in late. 8C1f

A. hardly never   C. don't never

B. nearly never   D. rarely

25. He has the _____handwriting in the class 8C1f

A. worse   C. bad

B. baddest   D. worst

26. Mike has decided to write a research paper on the origins of the vampire legend. Which one of the four questions below would best help him organize his paper? 8W1

A. Where do vampire bats live?

B. How many movies were made of the vampire legend?

C. Are there real vampires?

D. In which country did the first vampire legend appear?

In the following sentence, which words can be substituted for Brad and Britany.

27. Eric sat next to Brad and Britany.   8C1a

  A.   he and she   C.   he and her

  B.   him and her   D.   him and she

28. Choose the correct word to complete the sentence.   8C1a

> Daniel and _____ are preparing their speeches.

  A.   they   C.   me

  B.   him   D.   you

29.   8C1e

> The students had to _____their crayons on the teacher's desk.

  A.   lie   C.   laid

  B.   lay   D.   lain

30. Choose the sentence that contains an error.   8C1g

  A.   My grandmother warned me not to loose my jacket.

  B.   Every sentence should begin with a capital letter.

  C.   My clothes no longer fit me.

  D.   Atlanta is the capital of Georgia.

31. Choose the sentence that is written correctly.   8C1g

  A.   Does the schedule change effect us?

  B.   Texas boarders Mexico.

  C.   Tyrone lead the team onto the field.

  D.   The students were quiet while the teacher explained the problem.

32. Choose the sentence in which the underlined word is an error.   8C1g

  A.   <u>Whose</u> going to the concert tonight?

  B.   The <u>weather</u> is unpredictable.

  C.   Trying to change Chuck's mind is a <u>waste</u> of time.

  D.   <u>There</u> will be a meeting in the gym after school.

Select the sentence in each group that is incorrectly punctuated.   8C1g

33. A.   Thomas Edison once said, "Show me a thoroughly satisfied man — and I will show you a failure."

  B.   Abraham Lincoln once said that "voting power is greater than the power of a gun."

  C.   The dance instructor told all of her students, "Practice these exercises every day to be your best."

  D.   "In five years' time," the builder announced, "this land will be fully developed."

34. A.   Give me liberty or give me death! "was the war cry of the Revolutionary War."

  B.   "Turn around," commanded the king, "and I will show you the extent of my power."   8C1g

  C.   The aliens informed the humans that they were invading Earth in six days.

  D.   Shirley promised, "Give me two thousand dollars and in one month, I will redecorate your entire house."

35. A.   Kelly took the following with her: a CD player, suntan lotion, and a towel.

  B.   The basketball game starts at 7:00 p.m.

  C.   James needs the following items; a toothbrush, scissors, and a pair of socks.   8C1b

  D.   To Whom it May Concern:

Four of the five sentences in the box below make a paragraph. Read the sentences. Answer the questions below the box. **8W1**

> 1. This eruption preserved and hid the city of Pompeii for over 1,500 years.
>
> 2. The volcanoes of the Hawaiian Islands are very spectacular.
>
> 3. The ashes from the eruption covered the entire city.
>
> 4. Poisonous gas from the eruption killed most of the people of Pompeii within minutes.
>
> 5. Mt. Vesuvius erupted, sentencing the city of Pompeii to immediate death.

36. Which sentence is the best introductory sentence? **8W1**

A. Sentence 1   C. sentence 4

B. Sentence 3   D. sentence 5

37. Which sentence is the best concluding sentence? **8W1**

A. Sentence 1   C. Sentence 4

B. Sentence 2   D. Sentence 5

Identify the total number of underlined words that have capitalization errors.

38. The <u>student</u> asked, "<u>how</u> many times did <u>columbus</u> travel to the New <u>world</u>?" **8C1g**

A. one   C. three

B. two   D. four

39. Bill <u>Clinton</u> was the <u>President</u> of the <u>United States</u> for many years. **8C1g**

A. one   C. three

B. two   D. four

Select the correct word to replace the <u>underlined</u> part of the sentence.

40. The disc jockey played "Counting Blue Cars" for <u>Manny and I</u> at 5:35 p.m **8C1a**

A. us   C. our

B. we   D. they're

41. The 1969 Mustang always quits running when <u>the vehicle</u> has to make a sudden stop. **8C1a**

A. she   C. its

B. it   D. he

42. <u>Ken and Steve's</u> graduation pictures were available at the front office. **8C1a**

A. They're   C. There

B. Their   D. Them

Select the sentence fragment in each word group.

43. A. With one inning left and bases loaded.

B. I dropped the quarter into the machine.

C. Jake ran to the fire station and begged for their help. **8C1b**

D. Many people were concerned about the water shortage in their area.

44. A. Light was shining through the stained glass window. **8C1b**

B. Before I could pull the lever, the door closed.

C. As soon as we had the chance to leave the show.

D. Others left when the magic show was over.

Select the correct complete sentence in each word group. **8C1b**

45. A. Fred drove over the creek and breaking through the trees.

B. She ran to the car, her headlights were on.

C. The worker made the wood frame and poured the concrete.

D. Give me two guesses I'll tell you the answer.

46. A. The jungle was unusually quiet as we traveled through it. 8C1b

    B. People moved quickly there was no time to stop.

    C. One inning was left, bases were loaded.

    D. They hiked a mountain they saw a squirrel.

Select the run-on sentence in each word group.

47. A. Before I dressed for school, I called my best friend. 8C1b

    B. Both Nan and Don attend church meetings on Sunday nights.

    C. For her part in the play, she received an award for best leading actress.

    D. Terry flew to San Francisco, his camera was still in Mexico City.

48. A. The night was full of stars; it was very romantic. 8C1b

    B. We travel in circles there is no end in sight.

    C. It was snowing outside, so we decided to play Nintendo™.

    D. After the play, we went out for pizza.

---

1. The routine of a caravan on the march is as changeless as the desert itself.

2. The morning begins as a walk through the desert before the temperature is too hot.

3. In the afternoon, the Bedouins mount their camels and spare their bodies from overheating.

4. Nature has made sure this routine will not change for many years to come.

5. The tropical rain forest can reach high temperatures in the afternoon.

---

49. **Which sentence contains an unrelated idea?** 8W1

    A. Sentence 1 C. Sentence 2

    B. Sentence 4 D. Sentence 5

50. **Which sentence is the best concluding sentence?** 8W1

    A. Sentence 1 C. Sentence 3

    B. Sentence 4 D. Sentence 5

For questions 51 – 53, copy the following sentences adding all missing punctuation and correcting any capitalization errors.

51. **I cant meet you before 1100 oclock but that's probably too early for mr oconner.** 8C1g, 8C1e

52. **Dad offered me 20 to wash the car Saturday but Ill have ball practice.** 8C1e, 8C1g

53. **mr duffy our new french teacher graduated from georgia state university.** 8C1e, 8C1g

For questions 54 – 55, combine the sentences into one sentence. Be sure to punctuate and capitalize correctly.

54. **Jim is my little brother. He follows me around everywhere. I wish he could find his own friends to play with.** 8C1a, 8C1b

55. **My brother sent us a birthday present. Us never received it. Us wonder what it was.** 8C1a, 8C1b

For questions 56 – 60. Copy the sentences correcting dangling modifiers, unclear pronoun references, adverb, adjective, or verb errors.

56. **While shopping at the store last night, a wheel on my grocery cart fell off while I was pushing it through the store.** 8C1b

57. Kelly loved the jazz music of New
    Orleans and decided to become one. 8C1c

58. Christopher laughed very excited when
    he found out he won the race. 8C1f

59. Jasmina serves the ball quickly across the
    net yesterday at the tennis match. 8C1d

60. The frog stared at the approaching fly
    waiting for the right time to strike. 8C1c

For questions 61 – 65, answer the question or
follow the directions and write on your own
paper.

61. Name the reference source which would
    be most convenient for finding articles on
    gold, granite, and Georgia. 8W2

62. Rewrite this passage so each sentence is
    consistently from the first person point of
    view. 8W1

*I rode with my sister from the city to the lake. It was
his first time fishing with his sister. She liked to fish,
while you liked to skateboard.*

63. Write down two transition words you
    could use to contrast paper and plastic.
    8W4

64. Which part of a book should be used to
    find additional resources and supple-
    mentary information?

65. Read the chart following. What does the
    chart prove, if anything?

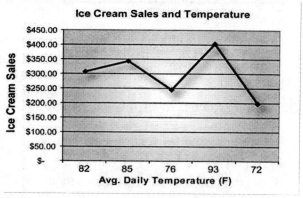

(Chart taken from Turner Hill Times article, "Summertime
Activity", 28 July 2005, Volume XXVII)

EVALUATION CHART FOR GEORGIA ENGLISH/LANGUAGE ARTS CRCT DIAGNOSTIC TEST

Directions: On the following chart, circle the question numbers that you answered incorrectly, and evaluate the results. These questions are based on the Georgia standards for reading and research. Then turn to the appropriate topics (listed by chapters), read the explanations, and complete the exercises. Review other chapters as needed. Finally, complete the practice test(s) to assess your progress and further prepare you for the CRCT.

*Note: Some question numbers will appear under multiple chapters because those questions require demonstration of multiple skills.

Chapters	Diagnostic Test Question
Chapter 1: Capitalization and Punctuation	4,10,19,20,33,34,35,38,39,51,52,53
Chapter 2: Nouns and Pronouns	6,8,11,15,27,28,40,41,42
Chapter 3: Verbs and Verbals	17,29,32,56,57,58,59,60,62
Chapter 4: Sentences/Subject-Verb Agreement	1,2,5,9,21,22,43,44,45,46,47,48,54,57,58,59,60
Chapter 5: Adjectives, Adverbs, Using Negative Words	16,18,22,23,24,25
Chapter 6: Sentence Errors and Sequencing	12,14
Chapter 7: Spelling	30,31,51,52,53
Chapter 8: Paragraphs	3,7,13,26,36,37,49,50,63
Chapter 9: Using Resource Materials	61,64,65

Chapter 1
Capitalization and Punctuation

This chapter references conventions	
ELA 8C1b	analyzes and uses simple, compound, complex, and compound-complex sentences correctly, punctuates properly, and avoids fragments and run-ons
ELA8C1e	demonstrates appropriate comma and semicolon usage (compound, complex, and compound-complex sentences, split dialogue, and for clarity)
ELA8C1g	produces final drafts/presentations that demonstrate accurate spelling and the correct use of punctuation and capitalization
ELA8W1	Writing Domain

CAPITALIZATION RULES

Rule 1. **Capitalize the first word of a sentence.**

> **Example 1:** **We** went to the candy store.

> **Example 2:** **When** will we be able to go swimming again?

Rule 2. **The first word of a sentence following a colon can begin with a small letter or a capital letter. Be consistent throughout your writing.**

> **Example 1:** Listen to the following announcement: **all** people living on planet Earth will now be ruled by aliens.

> **Example 2:** This is my question: **What** can I do to get out of debt?

Rule 3. **Capitalize the first word of a direct quotation that is a complete sentence, even if it is within another sentence.** When a quotation is interrupted by words such as *he said*, do not use a capital letter to begin the second part of the quotation.

> **Example 1:** Mr. White said, "**Be** here next Saturday at 9:00 a.m."

> **Example 2:** "Chrissy," said Joe, "**w**ill you be able to go with me?"

> **Example 3:** Erica moaned, "**We'll** be late if we don't leave right now," and left the room.

Rule 4. **Capitalize the pronoun *I* and the interjection *O*. Capitalize the word *oh* only when it appears at the beginning of a sentence.**

Example 1: Help us, **O** great one!

Example 2: **Oh**, I think **I** forgot my keys!

Example 3: It was, **oh**, so easy to ride the horse.

Rule 5. **Capitalize the names of specific persons, places, things, or ideas. Capitalize the adjectives that are formed from proper nouns.**

Example 1: **races and nationalities** – The food of **Asian** people is popular with **Canadians**.

Example 2: **geographical features** – When did you drive through the **Smoky Mountains**?

Example 3: **historical periods** – The **Great Awakening** was a time of religious fervor in **New England**.

Example 4: **titles of courses** – My **math** class is now **Introduction to Algebra**.

Example 5: **names of buildings, monuments, bridges** – I work in the **Freeman Center**.

Example 6: **names of celestial bodies** – **Saturn** is part of the **Milky Way**.

Example 7: **names of streets and roads** – He lives near **Wabash Street** and **Route 34**.

Example 8: **names of religions and terms for the sacred** – Most **Moslems** read the **Koran**.

Rule 6. **Capitalize the first letter of last names after the prefixes <u>D'</u>, <u>L'</u>, <u>O'</u>, <u>Mc</u>, and <u>Mac</u>.**

Example 1: Hetta **McFarland** drove me to school every day.

Example 2: I took Pamela **D'Ambrosio** with me to the school.

Example 3: Mr. **O'Hara** is the new math teacher.

Rule 7. **Capitalize compass directions only when they designate a specific region.**

Example 1: Gary Jones headed **south** because he wanted to explore the **Southwest**.

Example 2: We lived in the **Far East** and then settled in **West Texas**.

Example 3: Is Aunt Helen from the **South**?

Rule 8. **Capitalize family relationships only when they designate a specific person.**

Example 1: Did **Grandma** talk to my **uncle**?

Example 2: Did **Dad** buy my birthday present yet?

Example 3: Did you talk to my **dad** about it?

Practice 1: Capitalization Rules

Review rules 1 – 8. Then read the sentences below. Write a C if the sentence is correctly capitalized. Rewrite the sentence if the capitalization is incorrect.

1. Billy wrote, "i still haven't found what i'm looking for."

    _____

2. I heard that professor Jones headed south because he wanted to explore the southwest.

    _____

3. "The Summertime," said Steve, "Is my favorite time of year."

    _____

4. azaleas have been planted near the Martin Luther King center in atlanta, Georgia.

    _____

5. Mr. Mccoy was eating steak at the dixie diner.

    _____

6. Here is the verdict: the jury finds the defendant to be not guilty of all charges.

    _____

7. Did you tell Mother that we can get chinese food delivered now?

    _____

8. Barney Scott said, "the Pacific ocean is about two miles West of here."

    _____

9. The renaissance was a time when great art and thinking flourished.

    _____

10. All barbecue tastes better when it is made in the south.

    _____

Rule 9. **Capitalize every word in the titles of works of literature and film except articles (*a, an, the*), prepositions, conjunctions, and the *to* in infinitives. These rules apply unless the above parts of speech are the first or last words in the title.**

> **Example 1:** *Raiders of the Lost Ark*
>
> **Example 2:** *The Key to Ultimate Success*
>
> **Example 3:** *To Kill a Mockingbird*
>
> **Example 4:** *I Know Why the Caged Bird Sings*

Rule 10. Capitalize every word that appears in an address. Capitalize all letters in address abbreviations. If a period follows the abbreviation, capitalize only the first letter.

Example 1: PO Box 278

Santa Clara, CA 95050

Example 2: 4398 Shining Way Rd.

Vienna, Va. 22182-2285

Rule 11. Capitalize the name of every month and day of the week. Also, capitalize the word "day" if it appears after a holiday. However, do not capitalize the seasons.

Example 1: The storm began on **Wednesday, May** 12, 1992.

Example 2: Everyone is making plans for the **Labor Day** weekend.

Example 3: When is your **spring** vacation?

Rule 12. Capitalize titles that come before a proper name. Also capitalize abbreviations of names and titles.

Example 1: **Professor** Lowry is coming to the podium.

Example 2: Roy Lowry, a **professor**, is coming to the podium.

Example 3: My doctor's name is **T.J. McIntyre, M.D.**

Rule 13. Capitalize the first word and every noun of salutations and the first word of closings of letters.

Example 1: Dear Sir or Madam:

Example 2: Sincerely yours,

Rule 14. Capitalize the first word in every line where there is a numbered or lettered heading, such as an outline.

Example 1: I. Trees of the world

A. Trees native to the tropics

1. Palm trees

a. Date palms

Practice 2: More Capitalization Rules

Review rules 8 – 14. Then read the sentences below. Write a C if the sentence is correctly capitalized. Rewrite the sentence if the capitalization is incorrect.

1. The Chiropractor, dr. Lewis, adjusted the patient quickly and easily.

_____

2. The property for sale can be seen at 489 south main street.

_____

3. yours truly,

_____

4. Have you read Jack London's book, *The Call of the Wild*?

_____

5. I.   Powerful telescopes
   A. reflecting

_____

6. One of the most famous bankers in history is j.p. Morgan.

_____

7. Prince Charles gave the Bishop a plaque last friday for his work with the poor.

_____

8. The counselor in charge receives her mail at PO box 117, Red Oak, IA 51591.

_____

9. II. Freshwater Fish
    A. trout

_____

10. On september 16, Mexicans celebrate their independence from Spain.

_____

11. When we go back to school in the Fall, Mr. Bakersfield will be the Principal.

_____

12. Are you going anywhere for the Memorial day weekend?

_____

Practice 3: Capitalization Review

Review rules 1 – 14. Read the following sentences. Write a C if the sentence is correctly capitalized. Rewrite the sentence if the capitalization is incorrect.

1. after school, Rita and james decided to watch a spanish movie.

_____

2. My favorite classes in school are algebra I and Physical Science.

_____

3. Dear sir or madam:

   _____

4. My favorite character on *Star Trek* is captain Picard.

   _____

5. Trains traveling north should be wary of icy conditions.

   _____

6. The runner pleaded, "Please, give me a drink."

   _____

7. The children wanted to know: "Where does Santa Claus live?"

   _____

8. is father going to take care of uncle joe's garden?

   _____

9. In the Fall, you can plainly see the north star from the top of the Rocky mountains.

   _____

10. My birthday was on sunday, January 6, 1968.

    _____

11. Rejoice with me, o strongest of the strong!

    _____

12. I. Shakespeare
    A. the early years

    _____

13. This much is certain: Memorial day will be a federal holiday.

    _____

14. Write the letter to LaToya Ford, 278 Sherman Way, Houston, TX. 77017.

    _____

15. in the Winter, the average temperature is forty-five degrees.

    _____

16. "Not once in her life," tamara explained, "Did she ever allow us to take her picture."

_____

17. Have you seen *the return of the Jedi*?

_____

18. We saw doctor Freid treating a patient at Piedmont hospital.

_____

19. The address read, "4260 Starkley Avenue."

_____

20. Islam is the most prevalent religion in the arab world.

_____

PUNCTUATION RULES

COMMAS

Rule 1. Commas separate *independent clauses* (groups of words that form a coherent sentence) only when they are joined by a *conjunction* (words such as *and, but, or, nor, yet*).

Example 1: Jessie ran to the gas station, but he forgot his money.

Example 2: Renatta works at a copier center, and she has to stand up most of the time.

Rule 2. Commas are used to set *nonrestrictive elements* off from the rest of the sentence. Nonrestrictive elements are clauses, appositives, and phrases that are not essential to the meaning of the words they modify. *Restrictive elements*, on the other hand, are essential to the meaning of the words they modify and are *not* set off by commas.

Example 1: Nonrestrictive – The three adventurers involved in the rescue, **who were not afraid of risking their lives**, jumped into the pit to save their friend.

Example 2: Restrictive – The adventurers **who were not afraid of risking their lives** jumped into the pit to save their friend.

Example 3: Nonrestrictive – Darcie, **who is usually shy**, was the life of the party last night.

Example 4: Restrictive – **The football player who is usually shy** was the life of the party last night.

Example 5: Nonrestrictive – My father, **who was born in Tennessee**, is the youngest of five children.

Example 6: Restrictive – Anyone **who was born in Tennessee** is eligible to apply for the scholarship.

Rule 3. **Commas usually follow an introductory word, phrase, clause, or expression.**

    Example 1: **Besides,** the child was only six years old.

    Example 2: **By taking the lead,** Douglas infuriated his competitors.

    Example 3: **When I drive home from school,** I go right by your house.

Rule 4. **Commas are used to separate items in a series of three or more words, clauses, or phrases.**

    Example 1: **Frank, Charles, and Shirley** were all on phone restriction.

    Example 2: Thomas Dyer **played football, worked after school, and excelled in academics** as a teenager.

TIP

To determine when you use commas with items in a series, follow the rule of <u>and</u>. Insert <u>and</u> between adjectives, verbs, adverbs, or nouns. If the sentence makes sense with <u>and</u>, then the items in the series are coordinate and can be separated by commas. Otherwise, they are not separated by commas.

    Example 3: The principal found an updated Atlanta telephone book.

NOTE: In this case, the sentence does not make sense with *and* inserted, so the adjectives are not separated by commas.

    Example 4: The principal is fair, friendly, and tolerant.

NOTE: In this case, the sentence makes sense with the inserted *and*, so the adjectives can be separated by commas.

Practice 4: Punctuation Rules

Review rules 1– 4. Read the following sentences. Write a C if the sentence is correctly punctuated. Rewrite the sentence on the lines below if the sentence is incorrectly punctuated.

1. Jessie did not remember his name nor could he recognize his friends.

    _____

2. After all the woman hadn't promised to come to the party.

    _____

3. All people, who live west of the Chattahoochee River, are eligible for flood relief programs.

    _____

4. Mrs. Ringwald spoke read and wrote, about astronomy.

    _____

5. In case of fire Kelly installed smoke detectors, in each room of the house.

_____

6. Daniel Stern, a talented quarterback, scored the touchdown in twelve seconds.

_____

7. Stephanie tore ripped and chewed her way through the ropes before her captors returned.

_____

8. My uncle who was a prisoner, of war in Vietnam received an award from Congress.

_____

9. While the oven was hot Mom put in two more sheets of chocolate chip cookies.

_____

10. The cold dark cave which had never been explored was found by two boys playing in the woods.

_____

Rule 5. **Commas are used to set off added comments or information. Transitional expressions such as conjunctive adverbs are also set off with commas.**

   Example 1: My records, **however**, indicate that he paid his taxes every year.

   Example 2: Lyla, **as we know**, was out of the house when the fire started.

Rule 6. **Commas are used to set off direct address, tag questions, interjections, and opposing elements.**

   Direct Address Example: Carla, what is on the agenda today?

   Tag Question Example: We're not going in there, **are we**?

   Interjection Example: We drove across Tennessee, **surprisingly**, in one day.

   Opposing Elements Example: Rene was supportive, **not critical**, toward the project.

Rule 7. **Commas are used before and after quotations. Commas are not used when the quotation is a question, an interjection, an indirect quotation, or when the quotation includes the word** *that*.

   Example 1: "Go at once," **Gene commanded**, "and see what is causing that commotion."

   Example 2: Example 2: The lawyer says **that the trial system is fair.**

   Example 3: Example 3: People who say **"so long"** are using an expression.

Rule 8.   Commas are not used *after* a quotation when the quotation is an imperative or a question.

   Example 1: "You had better hand over that jacket, Mrs. Billings!" yelled the security guard.

   Example 2: "What are you doing here?" asked the baker.

Rule 9.   Commas are used between the date and year as well as after the year.

   Example: On December 3, 1995, Jessie got her wish.

Rule 10.   Commas are used after the street address or PO Box, city, and state in addresses. If the zip code is included, do not place a comma between the state and the zip code.

   Example 1: Greg Durham has lived at 627 LaVista Road, Novato, CA, for three years.

   Example 2: Candace Walker's new mailing address is PO Box 441, Orlando, FL 32887.

Practice 5: More Punctuation Rules

Review rules 5 – 10. Then read each sentence in this exercise. Rewrite each sentence that is incorrectly punctuated. Write C next to the sentence(s) that are correct.

1. Tammy told me, that she liked Robert and no one else.

   _____

2. "Daphne" Scooby said "I want a big turkey sandwich."

   _____

3. Lisa have you seen my gold-plated money clip?

   _____

4. You can write to Batman at PO Box 256, Gotham City NY 10018.

   _____

5. The wild birds eager to eat worms pecked at the ground in the forest.

   _____

6. "Did I really pass the medical exam," asked the student.

   _____

7. The arcade owner was shocked, not pleased, when he found out his business burned up last night.

   _____

8. When Mr. Lewis says "No," he means no.

   _____

9. She doesn't have to baby-sit tonight does she?

_____

10. Casper lives at 333 Carlsbad Avenue, Glendale, CA 91203.

_____

11. Marsha bumped her head, in fact, when she tried the roller coaster the first time.

_____

12. Puddy had her kittens on January 30 1994.

_____

Practice 6: Punctuation Review

Review rules 1 – 10 on punctuation. Read each of the sentences below. Write C if the sentence is correctly punctuated. Rewrite the sentences if there are errors in comma placement.

1. Feeling tired Rick and Jim went straight to bed.

_____

2. The two daughters Jenny and Allison were playing dolls during the storm.

_____

3. Cedrick opened the refrigerator, and found a pecan pie whipped cream and some milk.

_____

4. The pilot, full of fear, landed the plane on the dark icy runway.

_____

5. Just in time the train brought the needed supplies of food clothing and medicine.

_____

6. On January 17 1996 the concert tour began.

_____

7. "Angie did you find the puppy?" Sam's mother asked.

_____

8. The cereal as you know has passed its expiration date.

_____

9. Stasia a famous talented entertainer will be performing at The Apollo next week.

_____

10. "Give me five minutes" Cecil demanded "and I will tell you our plan of action."

_____

11. Michael Langston lives at 431 Baker Street Woodbury MN 55125

_____

12. The newspaper reported that the Nishon 627XT Camcorder has been recalled for lens defects.

_____

13. At that time the exterminator killed all the fleas ticks roaches and ants in the house.

_____

14. In that case, we won't attend the party or will we?

_____

15. Bernard Gray's work nevertheless was displayed at the Pinecrest Summer Exhibition.

_____

16. Rene Carter's wedding dress took in fact six weeks to complete.

_____

17. Sharon heard the joke and it made her laugh for hours.

_____

18. The politicians who were ready, for battle prepared their arguments for today's debates.

_____

19. The rabbits ran short medium and long distance races at the county fair.

_____

20. Skating to the bus Ina fell, and broke her kneecap.

_____

QUOTATION MARKS " "

Rule 1. Use quotation marks (" ") to signify a direct quotation.

Example 1: "Poor old tree!" said Dave, pointing to a crooked and gnarled elm standing by itself in the middle of a field.

Example 2: "Why Henry!" cried Ralph, jumping suddenly to his feet with surprise. "How did this happen?"

Rule 2. Use quotation marks (" ") to signify a short work of literature or a speech. Also, use single quotation marks (' ') when the title of a short work is inside a person's quotation.

Example 1: Martin Luther King's speech, "I Have a Dream," had a wide impact.

Example 2: Samuel Clemens wrote a story called "The Celebrated Jumping Frog of Calaveras County."

Example 3: "Have you read the story, 'The Lady or the Tiger?'" Holly asked.

Rule 3. Do *not* use quotation marks for indirect quotations because they do *not* contain someone's exact words. Conjunctions like *that, if, who, what,* and *why* often introduce indirect quotations.

Example 1: Jane said that she didn't want to go to the mall.

Example 2: Sylvia asked if the problem could wait until tomorrow.

Practice 7: Quotation Marks

Read the following sentences. Add quotation marks where needed. Write C if the sentence is correct.

1. Halt! cried the old hero. Who goes there?

_____

2. Chad said that the engine would not last another week.

_____

3. Arnold wrote in the school newspaper that the protest is growing.

_____

4. The trainer said to the gorilla, bring me a banana.

_____

5. In that case, Tricia remarked, please buy me another video tape.

_____

6. Don't you think they ought to let me leave? Keisha said with a homesick look.

_____

7. Daniel explained why the toll booth was out of order on Highway 400.

_____

8. Well, Jennifer announced, my boyfriend is not here yet.

_____

9. You asserted that Gabe was responsible for the accident.

_____

10. Kevin stated that he would never set foot in that place again.

_____

COLONS

Rule 1.   Use a colon to introduce a list, series, quotation, or formal statement.

    Example 1: The following answers are possible: a, b, c, or all of the above.

    Example 2: At some time in your life, you will ask the question: Why do I exist?

Rule 2.   Use a colon before a second independent clause which restates or explains the first clause.

    Example: The singer had a great voice: every tone that she sang was in tune with the music.

Rule 3.   Use a colon after a greeting in a formal business letter.

    Example 1: Dear Sir or Madam:

    Example 2: To Whom It May Concern:

Rule 4.   Use a colon to separate chapters and verses in the Bible and to separate hours and minutes.

    Example 1: The answer can be found in Acts 2:38.

    Example 2: This movie gets out at 2:43 p.m.

Practice 8: Colons

Read the following sentences, and add colons where they are needed.

1.   Shakespeare stated the problem best "To be or not to be. That is the question."

_____

2. Theresa was a great swimmer her body barely made a splash when she dived.

_____

3. These three remained on the list Anne Richards, Kelly Joyce, and Fred Wilson.

_____

4. By then, the facts were obvious Mrs. Reid and Mr. Fannin had received the promotions.

_____

5. The store closes at 1030 p.m.

_____

6. In the newspaper, the farmer read this statement All land east of Talanachi Mountain will be taxed annually by order of the county at a rate of 2% of the assessed land value.

_____

_____

7. John 1 1 states "In the beginning was the Word and the Word was with God and the Word was God." -NIV

_____

8. High school graduates have the same concerns What will I do when I graduate? Will I continue living at home? What kind of jobs can I get?

_____

9. I need to bring four items to class my textbook, my notebook, my calculator, and my pencils.

_____

10. Three years later, the skaters read this sign in the city park No skateboarding allowed.

_____

SEMICOLONS ;

Rule 1. **Semicolons separate independent clauses that are *not* joined by a conjunction. Usually, semicolons are used in place of periods when the two independent clauses are closely related.**

Example: The saleswoman sold two houses; she was very happy that day.

Rule 2. Semicolons separate independent clauses that are joined by sentence interrupters (for instance, nevertheless, besides, moreover, instead, besides, and so on).

    Example: The people were panicking in the streets; nevertheless, the ambulance was able to move through the crowds.

Rule 3. Semicolons are sometimes used to split independent clauses when there are several commas inside the clauses.

    Example: Mr. Trump, a writer, announced his new horror, mystery, and science fiction series; yet the books, oddly enough, had not been written.

Rule 4. Semicolons are used if a colon precedes items in a series.

    Example: These athletes were all participating in the national competition: Judy Dawes, a world class diver; Joe Chung, a champion weight lifter; and Sherry Whittaker, an Olympic gymnast.

Practice 9: Semicolons

Read the following sentences and correctly add semicolons. Write C if the sentence is correct.

1. Carlos wouldn't have stolen from anyone besides, he was on vacation at the time.

   _____

2. The stainless steel rake was used in the garden nevertheless, no one used it to rake leaves.

   _____

3. The following people were involved in helping the child: Jerry MacDonald, a nutritionist, Tanya Steinem, a physical therapist and Rick Plucheck, a pediatrician.

   _____

   _____

4. The captain brought the ship into port the sailors unloaded the supplies.

   _____

5. After finishing her breakfast, Susan noticed her speakers, television, and stereo were missing strange as it may seem, the front door was locked, and the alarm system showed no record of forced entry.

   _____

   _____

6. Christie Williams, president of the senior class, was trying to change the lunch room, tardy passes, and dress code policies at her school because of her enthusiasm, she got the changes she wanted.

   _____

   _____

   _____

7. The choir members left the rehearsal the choir director, however, stayed behind.

   _____

8. The coach depended on these players in the last quarter of the football game: Dan Chisolm, the quarterback Rod Curtis, the wide receiver and Terrell Jones, the running back.

   _____

   _____

9. Cold air blew through the mine shaft the mine lights shattered in the gust.

   _____

10. The people were distracted by the loud music besides, the incident happened at night.

    _____

USING APOSTROPHES IN CONTRACTIONS AND OTHER OMISSIONS

Rule 1. **Contractions are combinations of two words that leave out certain letters.** The places for the missing letters are marked with apostrophes (').

The following is a list of common contractions:

I am / I'm	you are / you're	she is, she has / she's
would not / wouldn't	it is / it's	there had / there'd
all is / all's	do not / don't	who is, who has / who's
I would, I had / I'd	cannot / can't	we will / we'll
let us / let's	will not / won't	is not / isn't
did not / didn't	I have / I've	who will / who'll
are not / aren't	there is / there's	we would, we had / we'd
they are / they're	he will / he'll	she will / she'll
would have / would've	should have / should've	could have / could've
should not / shouldn't	could not / couldn't	we are / we're

Rule 2. The words *it is* are contracted as *it's*. However, if *it* acts as a possessive pronoun, the word changes to *its*.

    Example 1: It's going to be a great day!

    Example 2: Make sure the dog eats **its** food while we're gone.

Rule 3. Apostrophes can signal omissions in phrases.

    Example 1: rock and roll / rock 'n' roll

    Example 2: six of the clock / six o'clock

Rule 4. Apostrophes can be used to make the plural form of letters, symbols, numbers, and term words.

    Example 1: The typewriter cannot print letter *j*'s very well.

    Example 2: All of the $'s were put in the wrong place in the tax report.

    Example 3: The 7's became 2's when the message was decoded.

    Example 4: The warriors' *huzza's* grew louder as the day continued.

Practice 10: Apostrophes

Read the following sentences. Correct the mistakes using apostrophes. Use contractions whenever possible. If the sentence is correct, write C on the line.

1. Theyre all scared that its going to rain tomorrow.

    _____

2. What Alice does'nt know cannot hurt her.

    _____

3. If Damon will not quit smoking cigarettes, Im leaving the house.

    _____

4. Hes certain that his allergies are'nt the problem.

    _____

5. The car wreck could have been fatal if Jessie hadnt worn her seat belt.

    _____

6. All of you should eat this barbecue; its really good!

    _____

7. Its six oclock and alls well.

    _____

8. Jessica Stern should've made the %'s a half space lower on this page.

_____

9. Frank says he will not ride her ten speed when shes not here.

_____

10. Our leader decided we would help these kids since they couldnt help themselves.

_____

11. Who'l make sure that all of the *and*s in this story are correctly spelled?

_____

12. Lets go to the farm, and we will feed the animals.

_____

13. Its going to fall if we dont add supports to the building.

_____

14. You will be an entertainer who is going to influence many people.

_____

15. There had better be some grade improvement, or Il'l put you on phone restriction.

_____

16. All 3s, please form a single-file line so we will be ready to load the bus.

_____

17. They've really shown us that they're responsible on their own.

_____

18. Alls well that ends well.

_____

19. Youre positive you were not in the office at the time of the accident?

_____

20. Id like to buy the CD player, but I will not have the money until Thursday.

_____

END PUNCTUATION

Rule 1.   **A period comes after a complete statement.**
        Example: The telescope had a convex lens**.**

Rule 2.   **A question mark comes after any question.**
        Example: Where is the jar of pickles**?**

Rule 3.   **An exclamation point follows an emotional or forceful statement.**
        Example: That hot oil is burning my hand**!**

Practice 11: End Punctuation

Read the following, and add the appropriate end punctuation.

1. Wash these filthy dishes now

2. I just won a trip to Disney World

3. Where does your friend live

4. Who do you think will win the election

5. My little sister doesn't know how to draw a picture

6. Trout can be found in freshwater lakes, rivers, and streams

7. I just won a million dollars in the sweepstakes

8. Why should Jake go to college

9. Hey, what are you doing in my house

10. They think they can stay here tonight

11. I wonder what we're having for dinner

12. Will I ever see you again

13. Open the door quickly

14. I can't remember whether Sonya stayed home or went to school

15. You just ate a fly

16. What are you looking for

17. Open the test booklet, and begin reading

18. Do your best in school, and you will have success in life

19. How would he like going to the movies tomorrow

20. Tammy told me about your new computer

Copyright American Book Company. DO NOT DUPLICATE. 1-888-264-5877

CHAPTER 1 REVIEW

In the following sentences, correct any capitalization or punctuation errors. If the sentence is correct, write C on the line.

1. Late on Saturday night Charles and Susan drove to the concert they had just enough money to buy the tickets

   _____

   _____

2. The zoo had the following animals in cages lions tigers and bears

   _____

3. Molly told the doctor, I'm going to get a second opinion.

   _____

4. Just in time for christmas the store placed all the winter clothes on sale

   _____

5. The team was very diverse a police woman a minister and a professional weight lifter were called in for the exercises

   _____

   _____

6. The following journalists were in the courtroom: Lana Scarsborough, channel 5 news Trish Cleary, WZDX radio and Ken Stanway, channel 8 news.

   _____

   _____

7. Could you please show me how this works, asked the secretary.

   _____

8. On November 21 2004, your swiss bank account will have eighty-thousand dollars.

   _____

9. If you go South of Mobile Alabama by car, youl'l end up at the beach.

   _____

10. If we have perfect attendance this semester can we drop the final exam.

_____

11. with no time to spare Jessie drove to the stadium

_____

12. Mrs. Caloric screamed "this coffee's burning my tongue"

_____

13. After all that work, "Chris asked," why did you decide to quit?

_____

14. One important question might be how does this relate to my career

_____

15. All of this studying i assume will help me pass this Test.

_____

16. Wait a minute! She screamed I think Ive found the answer.

_____

17. Tom bought a pair of shoes today however both shoes were for the left foot

_____

18. Doreen, Carrie, and Allison asked for a new type of hand brake

_____

19. The show started early as a result most of the audience missed the beginning of the performance.

_____

20. West Oak High School, which I didn't attend, is now a warehouse.

_____

21. The girl in the red dress is my only sister kelli.

_____

22. mother stayed here in the south but dad moved up north to Chicago.

_____

23. Bill Cosby who has several college degrees is one of the most popular entertainers

_____

24. She will finish chapter 4 in her science book at 2 45 p.m.

_____

25. Gerald took the children to the amusement park I stayed home and cooked dinner.

_____

CHAPTER 1 TEST

Read carefully, and select the best answer to each question.

For questions 1 – 8, circle the letter which contains an error in capitalization within its line.

1.
A.	Quebec is a canadian	C.	of the U.S. border.
B.	province located north	D.	no mistakes

2.
A.	Jack Means has lived	C.	for most of his life.
B.	at 267 Stanton ave.	D.	no mistakes

3.
A.	The student asked, "how	C.	travel to the New World?"
B.	many times did Columbus	D.	no mistakes

4.
A.	Mr. Tucker has been	C.	Airlines for many years.
B.	the President of the Southern	D.	no mistakes

5.
A.	Mr. Krenshaw, a renouned journalist	C.	at the funeral.
B.	was seated next to Deacon Powers	D.	no mistakes

6.
A.	This day was, i believe,	C.	victory over Germany.
B.	very important for the allied	D.	no mistakes

7.
A.	Archie, a rat who lost his hearing,	C.	when the Jazz music played.
B.	scurried inside the piano	D.	no mistakes

8.
A.	George Lucas's movie	C.	was a rousing hit at the movies.
B.	*Return of The Jedi*,	D.	no mistakes

For questions 9 – 16, circle the letter that contains an error in punctuation within its line.

9.
A. The woman asked,
B. "Are you sure there arent
C. any bathrooms on this floor?"
D. no mistakes

10.
A. Did Jan take Dave, Kenneth,
B. Stephanie, and Courtney
C. with her to the concert.
D. no mistakes

11.
A. Teri and Mark went to the park,
B. in-line skates in hand,
C. to skate in a race.
D. no mistakes

12.
A. "You should have
B. given the money to me,"
C. Jan's mother said.
D. no mistakes

13.
A. The woman screamed!
B. "Stop! Give me back
C. my purse, you thief!"
D. no mistakes

14.
A. Did Jeff return the VCR,
B. the camcorder, and the
C. stereo system to you?
D. no mistakes

15.
A. Joseph sat down
B. brought out his notebook,
C. and took notes during his teacher's lec-ture.
D. no mistakes

16.
A. "There was a German Shepherd reported
B. missing at 369 5th Ave yesterday."
C. said the policeman.
D. no mistakes

Select the sentence in each group that is *incorrectly* punctuated.

17. A. Every person in this nation has the following rights: life, liberty, and the pursuit of happiness.

 B. Did you visit Ramon in the hospital?

 C. At 245 p.m., my flight is scheduled to begin boarding.

 D. My favorite foods are as follows: pizza, lasagna, and roast beef.

18. A. "If you want to win," the coach said, "you have to pay the price for winning."

 B. "Attention! Forward march!" yelled the drill sergeant.

 C. Martha Dwire says that these people are'nt very intelligent.

 D. The sign in the restaurant read, "No smoking, please."

19. A. You must have the following in your possession: your passport, your visa, and your baggage.

 B. The ingredients for this recipe are as follows; one cup peanut butter, one cup corn syrup, one cup sugar, and five cups crispy rice cereal.

 C. Shandra, make sure you take your keys.

 D. The funeral will begin at 10:00 a.m.

20. A. Samuel Johnson once said that "it doesn't matter how you die but how you live."

 B. "Bring the video tapes with you," her father commanded.

 C. "By the time I arrived, the crime had been committed," the witness stated.

 D. The doorman asked, "Could I help you with those packages?"

21. A. Their activities included the following: playing capture the flag, telling ghost stories, and building a campfire.

 B. The train arrived promptly at 7:30 p.m.

 C. These responsibilities fell on Georgette: washing the car, feeding the dog, and watering the plants.

 D. We ordered two pizzas from Pappa Dons Restaurant.

22. A. Candace Stone brought me to my appointment at 4:25 p.m.

 B. Shawn Kirklin has the following tasks to accomplish: stamping, sealing, and mailing the envelopes.

 C. Pablo Jimenez performed as follows; in biology, he received an A, in German, he received a B+, and in weight lifting, he received a B-.

 D. At 4:25 p.m., my favorite program comes on television.

23.　A. Abraham Lincoln began the Gettysburg Address by saying, "Four score and seven years ago…"

　　　B. "Even so," Carrie began, "I still do not believe that Sherrie committed the crime."

　　　C. Did Greg really say that we are playing his CD choices on the radio this month?

　　　D. If I could get another job, I would do it, Terry said.

24.　A. "Just give me one more chance, and I will show you what I need," Stacy said.

　　　B. "If she had the right tools, Andy said, I could help her more effectively."

　　　C. Albert Camus once said, "You cannot create experience. You must undergo it."

　　　D. "If I had a dollar for every time I've lost my keys," Mark said, "I'd be a rich man."

25.　A. Make sure the baby drinks her formula.

　　　B. If it's cold outside, we'll move the picnic indoors.

　　　C. During the time I was in Florida my car was stolen.

　　　D. How many of your friends ride the bus to school each day?

Chapter 2
Nouns and Pronouns

This chapter references conventions	
ELA 8C1a	declines pronouns by gender and case, and demonstrates correct usage in sentences
ELA8C1g	produces final drafts/presentations that demonstrate accurate spelling and the correct use of punctuation and capitalization

NOUNS

A **noun** is a word representing a person, place, thing, idea, animal, quality, or action such as **Jack, town, Venetian glass, wisdom, goose, excellence, arrival**. Nouns and words acting as nouns are the subjects and objects of sentences. They usually change in spelling to indicate the plural and possessive forms. **Examples include: woman, women, woman's, women's, town, towns, arrival, arrivals.**

There are two types of nouns: **proper** and **common**.

Proper nouns are nouns which refer to specific persons, places, things, ideas, or animals. They are always capitalized.

> **Examples: Jackie Robinson, Alaska, Big Mac™, Heimlich maneuver, Lassie.**

Common nouns are nouns which refer generally to persons, places, things, ideas, animals, qualities, or actions. These words are not capitalized *unless* they appear at the beginning of the sentence.

> **Examples:** left-handers, lake, pipe organ, anger, innocence, operation, jaguars.

Practice 1: Common and Proper Nouns

Read the following sentences. Underline all common nouns <u>once</u> and all proper nouns <u>twice</u>.

> **Example:** <u>Casey</u> took a new <u>job</u> in the <u>Twin Cities</u>.

1. Lyle loves to see his favorite singer, Bodo, in concert.

2. Blain ran all of the activities during the church lock-in.

3. Frank and his cousin, Artie, spent the day watching the latest movies.

4. Selena was known as a rising star before she was killed by one of her employees.

5. The wrestling team is putting its athletes on a strict diet to be at the top of their weight class.

6. Our color guard instructor is very good at maintaining discipline with our whole group.

7. "Jefferson High School's football coach is making you do too many pushups," Terry said.

8. For my birthday, I asked Major Flores for a ride in his hot air balloon.

9. "You need to sit up straight in your seats!" the music teacher said to the students.

10. All the best achieving students joined the Beta Club.

11. For the first time, Jim Dedashdi was able to order a meal without needing a translator.

12. In the potato sack race, my sister fell over the master-of-ceremonies.

13. Andy takes time every day to bike around the neighborhood.

14. Alex found the answer to his homework assignment on the internet.

15. There will be a racquetball court at our school next year.

NOUNS: SINGULAR AND PLURAL

A **noun** is a word that represents a **person**, **place**, **thing**, or **idea**. Each noun has two forms based on number.

A **singular noun** is a word that represents one person, place, thing, or idea.

A **plural noun** is a word that represents more than one person, place, thing, or idea. There are many rules associated with making nouns plural.

PLURAL RULES

Rule 1.   **Most nouns form plurals by adding s.**

> **Examples:** finger, fingers, cat, cats

Rule 2.   **Nouns ending in o form the plural by adding es as long as o is preceded by a consonant.**

> **Examples:** domino, dominoes, torpedo, torpedoes

Rule 3.   **Nouns ending in s, ch, sh, x, or z are made plural by adding es.**

> **Examples:** gas, gases, rich, riches, dish dishes, box, boxes, fez, fezes

Rule 4.   **Most nouns that end in f or fe form the plural by changing the f to a v and adding es.**

> **Examples:** wolf, wolves, half, halves, life, lives

Rule 5.   Nouns that end with the letters <u>is</u> form the plural by adding an <u>e</u> in place of the <u>i</u>.

  Examples: basis, bas**es**, crisis, cris**es**

Rule 6.   Nouns that end with the letters <u>us</u> can be made plural by adding <u>es</u> to the end of the word. Sometimes, however, the words are made plural by substituting <u>i</u> for <u>us</u>.

  Examples: cactus, cact**i**, focus, foc**i**, bus, bus**es**

Rule 7.   Nouns that end in <u>y</u> are made plural by replacing the <u>y</u> with <u>ies</u> only if preceded by a <u>consonant</u>.

  Examples: cherry, cherr**ies**, story, stor**ies**, way, way**s**, boy, boy**s**

Rule 8.   Some words do not change spellings between the singular and plural forms.

  Examples: one deer, five deer; one sheep, five sheep.

Practice 2: Singular and Plural Nouns

Read the following list. Next to the singular words, write the plural form.

Singular	Plural	Singular	Plural
1. frame	_____	11. story	_____
2. octopus	_____	12. elephant	_____
3. tornado	_____	13. alumnus	_____
4. popcorn	_____	14. calf	_____
5. crop	_____	15. berry	_____
6. trench	_____	16. wife	_____
7. ferry	_____	17. play	_____
8. flesh	_____	18. taste	_____
9. tax	_____	19. shelf	_____
10. wish	_____	20. potato	_____

COLLECTIVE NOUNS

Some nouns name a group of people or things. A **herd** of cows, for instance, refers to a group of cows. "The **band** will play," refers to a group of musicians.

On the next page is a list of commonly used collective nouns.

army	collection	group	public
assembly	committee	herd	school
audience	company	jury	society
band	crew	navy	swarm
board	crowd	number	team
chorus	family	orchestra	tribe
class	flock	pack	troop
club	government	panel	

Practice 3: Collective Nouns

From each group of words below, underline the collective noun.

1. sound	pack	goose	intelligence	plant
2. nature	girl	navy	future	magazine
3. audience	onion	joy	clocks	belt
4. jury	capsule	goats	traveler	mother
5. geese	collection	bushel	garden	books
6. map	wind	codes	team	fence
7. class	library	airport	calculator	hoop
8. zoo	barn	crew	rain	floor
9. plans	trouble	computer	family	collage
10. horses	assembly	cards	notebook	activity

RULES FOR MAKING NOUNS POSSESSIVE

A **possessive noun** is a noun which shows ownership, possession, or attachment.

Rule 1. To make singular nouns possessive, add an apostrophe (') and an <u>s</u>.

 Examples: Sarah**'s** idea   the cat**'s** water bowl

Rule 2. If the singular noun ends with an <u>s</u>, add an apostrophe and an <u>s</u>.

 Examples: the boss**'s** best employee   the heiress**'s** fortune

Rule 3. To make a plural noun ending in <u>s</u> possessive, add only the apostrophe.

 Examples: the three boys**'** toy train   the Keckleys**'** residence

Rule 4. **If a plural noun does not end in <u>s</u>, the word is made possessive by adding an apostrophe and an <u>s</u>.**

    Examples: the women**'s** gym   the sheep**'s** food supply

Rule 5. **For compound words, make the last word in the group possessive.**

    Examples: my son-in-law**'s** birthday

                   the master-of-ceremony**'s** speech

Rule 6. **To show personal possession by two or more owners, make each noun possessive. To show joint possession of the same object, make only the last noun possessive.**

    Examples: Whitney Houston**'s** and Dolly Parton**'s** singing styles are very different.

                   Dawn and Kent**'s** dad will be coming home tomorrow.

Practice 4: Possessive Nouns

Rewrite the following sentences. Decide how each boldfaced word should be changed to show possession.

1. **Tom Carney and his two sons** health club is large and has over two hundred members.

   _____

2. The **ladies** night out was a complete success.

   _____

3. **Mr. Landiss** tractor was very useful on the farm.

   _____

4. In the park, the two **elephants** bellows caused a stampede.

   _____

5. In order to mature correctly, **human beings** diets must be continually regulated.

   _____

6. During the formal questioning, the **foreigners** accent proclaimed his country of origin.

   _____

7. As the concert continued, the **fans** yells became louder than the music.

   _____

8. The **press** call for more freedom from government control was ignored.

   _____

9. Coming in red, pink, and purple, the **cotton candies** colors made them more desirable.

_____

10. Flying over Greenland, the airplane was controlled by the **pilots** computer.

_____

11. My **brother-in-laws** gift was very expensive.

_____

12. **Sojourner Truths** quest for **womens** rights was similar to **Elizabeth Cady Stantons**.

_____

PRONOUN FORMS

A pronoun is a word that takes the place of a noun. Words such as **I, we, us, them, their,** and **you** are all examples of pronouns.

There are three basic types of pronouns: **nominative, objective,** and **possessive.**

A. Nominative pronouns are used whenever a pronoun is used as a subject.

> **Example:** Amy and **I** are going water skiing.
> In this example, **I** is part of the subject, so the pronoun **I** has to be nominative.

B. Objective pronouns are used when the pronoun answers the questions, "What?" or "Whom?" after the action verb.

> **Example:** I heard **him** in the courtyard.
> In this example, **him** answers the question, "Heard Whom?" so the pronoun is in the objective case.

C. Possessive pronouns are used to show ownership or attachment.

> **Example:** **His** watch is very expensive.
> In this example, **His** answers the question: Who owns the watch?

Personal Pronoun Forms		
Nominative	**Objective**	**Possessive**
I	me	my, mine
you	you	your, yours
she	her	her, hers
he	him	his
it	it	its
we	us	our, ours
they	them	their, theirs
who	whom	whose
whoever	whomever	

NOTE: Some people confuse their pronouns. Remember how the pronoun is used in the sentence to determine the correct form.

> **Example:** Carlotta and me are going swimming today.
> In this sentence, **me** is incorrectly used. Because the pronoun is part of the subject, it is a nominative pronoun. **I** should replace me.

Practice 5: Pronoun Forms

Read the following sentences. If the bolded word is correctly used in the sentence, write C. If the word is not correct, rewrite the sentence with the correct pronoun.

1. **Her** and I went to the mall during the Back-to-School Sale.

   _____

2. We were competing with **them** for the prize.

   _____

3. The people had **us'** belongings placed on the ship.

   _____

4. Kelly asked Randall and **he** to help her in the kitchen.

   _____

5. Stan didn't realize the television was **hers**.

   _____

6. The pocket watch had **it's** centerpiece taken out for repairs.

_____

7. **Who** did Sylvia dance with?

_____

8. This is **him** who is speaking.

_____

9. Please relay the message to **she.**

_____

10. Just in time, the cook baked food for **we.**

_____

PRONOUN AGREEMENT

A pronoun should refer to *one* clear noun coming before the pronoun. The noun is the pronoun's **antecedent**.

antecedent ◄──────── pronoun

Example 1: Before we visited the **Smoky Mountains**, we studied **them** in our science class.
In Example 1, **them** refers to the antecedent, **Smoky Mountains**.

antecedent ◄──────── pronoun

Example 2: **Paula** cleaned **her** room after the party.
In Example 2, **her** refers to the antecedent, **Paula**.

Practice 6: Pronouns and Antecedents

Read the following sentences. Draw an arrow from each pronoun to its antecedent. Correct any errors in pronoun case. Write C next to any correct sentences.

◄──────── they

Example: Although the plums were ripe, it tasted bitter.

1. The trees were very beautiful in the fall; them were turning red and yellow.

2. Before Rita consented to the operation, she was given time to decide.

3. We decided to give Rhonda everything her wanted.

4. The mountains are a great place to visit, and they have some of the best tourist areas in the state.

5. Seven states can be seen from Lookout Mountain when it is not covered with clouds.

6. Carlos has a used truck, and their wheels need an alignment.

7. Carmen gave the keys to his friends because he trusted him.

8. The banjo is very popular in country music because of their twangy sound.

9. Mother works hard raising the family, and her often goes without sleep when the children cry.

10. Eastern Tennessee is full of caves for exploration, and it often contains bats during some weeks in the year.

11. Carla Polk, Lester Thompson, and I were at the scene of the car accident because us are all emergency medical technicians.

12. Because of its beautiful feathers, many birds have been hunted to extinction.

Sometimes the antecedent of a pronoun is not clear.

> **Example 1: Take** the dish out of the refrigerator and clean it.

What does the **it** refer to? Is someone supposed to clean the dish or the refrigerator? You could take it both ways. This is known as a **faulty pronoun reference.**

Sometimes the word the pronoun refers to is used as an adjective rather than a noun.

> **Example 2:** The popcorn bag was empty, but we were tired of eating it anyway.

Common sense tells you they were eating the popcorn, not the bag. But in this sentence, popcorn is used as an adjective describing the bag, so **it** cannot refer to the popcorn, **it** must refer to a noun. This is another type of **faulty pronoun reference.**

Sometimes there is no antecedent at all.

> **Example 3:** It said on the news that school is closed Monday. We have no idea what **it** refers to. This is also a faulty pronoun reference.

The best way to fix these sentences is to replace the pronoun with a noun.

     Example 1: Take the dish out of the refrigerator and clean the dish.

     Example 2: The popcorn bag was empty, but we were tired of eating popcorn anyway.

     Example 3: The weatherman said on the news that school is closed Monday.

Practice 7: Pronoun Reference

Each of the sentences below has a faulty pronoun reference. Rewrite each sentence to make the meaning clear.

1. When Orlando saw the accident, he called the television station but they didn't respond.

2. The clothes basket was empty because they were in the dryer.

3. I will take the belt off the dress and fix it.

4. Mary called Pricilla's house all day but no one ever answered it.

5. The boys carried the couch out of the living room and cleaned it.

6. In the middle of her paper, it describes the old house.

7. The fruit plate was clean because we had eaten it.

8. On most television shows, they present false ideas about life.

9. Traci gave the speech before, but it was not loud enough.

10. Neither the teacher nor the student has yet told her side of the story.

11. The elephant stood beneath the tree; it was old and weak.

12. Emily told her she looked good in red.

13. I told my brother that I was going to visit John which angered my mother.

14. When Joe feeds the dog, he eats too much.

15. At the end of the movie they are saved from drowning.

16. They say Christmas will be here before you know it.

17. It said on the radio this morning it will be 100 degrees today.

18. It was a wonderful day.

DEMONSTRATIVE PRONOUNS AND ADJECTIVES

This, *that*, *these*, and *those* are **demonstrative words** that can be used as either pronouns or adjectives. Demonstrative words are used to point out specific persons, places, things, or ideas. When they are used alone, they are **demonstrative pronouns**.

This is used to point out a singular object that is close by.

Example: **This** tastes very good!

These is used to point out plural objects that are close by.

Example: **These** are the only doughnuts we have left.

That is used to point out a singular object far away.

Example: **That** is my book over there by the door.

Those is used to point out plural objects that are far away.

Example: "Heidi, can you pick **those** up and bring them here?" her father asked.

This, *that*, *these*, and *those* can also be used as adjectives. They are demonstrative adjectives when they are followed by the noun they describe.

Example: **This** hamburger tastes very good.

Example: **These** doughnuts are the only ones we have left.

Example: Do you see **that** book over there by the door?

Example: "Heidi, can you pick up **those** fishing poles and bring them here?" her father asked.

Practice 8: Demonstrative Pronouns and Adjectives

Read the following sentences. Fill in the blank with the appropriate demonstrative pronoun or demonstrative adjective.

1. _____ doors over there could use another coat of paint.

2. I am going to sell _____ motorcycle of yours.

3. "Bart, could you take _____ out of my hands?" his father said.

4. "We have to take _____ dog over there to the veterinarian," the boy said to his mother.

5. Jade and her friend, Blaze, spent _____ dollars as soon as they got them.

6. "The support of _____ group has helped me immensely!" Phillip said at the meeting.

7. Faye, Luke, and Laura wrote _____ songs in my studio.

8. Roger Bernal pointed to a far away tree and said, "_____ is a sycamore."

9. Tim and Benjamin are the only people who clean _____ kitchen in the next building.

10. Judith and Terry are going to tie the knot _____ coming Saturday at 10:00 a.m.

INDEFINITE PRONOUNS AND ADJECTIVES

An **indefinite pronoun** is a word which stands for something that is unknown in **meaning or quantity**. For example, the word **all** does not indicate the number of things that together make *all*. Some indefinite pronouns are used in the singular sense, such as **any**. Other words are used in the plural sense, such as **many**.

Examples: **All** are welcome at our church. **Many** stayed at home this weekend.

Here is a list of indefinite pronouns:

all	another	any	anybody	anyone	anything
both	each	either	everybody	everyone	everything
few	*half	many	somebody	most	much
neither	nobody	none	something	nothing	**one
several	some	more	someone	no one	other (s)

*any fractions   **any numerals

Like demonstrative pronouns, **indefinite pronouns** can also be used as indefinite adjectives when they are followed by the noun they describe. **Example:** *Most* cars come with a warranty.

Practice 9: Indefinite Pronouns and Adjectives

Read the following sentences, and write the indefinite pronouns or adjectives in each sentence.

1. Cassandra is selling the most jewelry in her department.

   _____

2. At the wedding, everyone was interested in two persons — the bride and the groom.

   _____

3. For many months, something seemed different about Jeremy.

   _____

4. As a present for Martha, I sent her something no one else would have thought of.

   _____

5. When you have to change schools, many adjustments are necessary.

   _____

6. Both Joey and his friend, Dennis, took a trip down to the river to play hide-and-seek.

   _____

7. The bird flew off of Ty Ling's finger and built a nest several miles away.

_____

8. For much of the year, one-fourth of the students in our school are in trailers.

_____

9. Few know more about making a good friendship than Jodi.

_____

10. We would need many more gallons of water to completely fill this pool.

_____

11. Gary and Tina spent the whole afternoon trying to bring others to their cause.

_____

12. Anybody could have taken her purse from the classroom.

_____

13. Have you spoken to anyone about anything you saw?

_____

14. What did Cassie and Fred do with the other science textbooks?

_____

15. No one has given those three students any of their money for the new sneakers.

_____

RELATIVE AND INTERROGATIVE PRONOUNS

Relative pronouns are words that act as a connection in a sentence. They begin a dependent clause and link it to an independent clause in the same sentence. There are five relative pronouns: *that, which, who, whom, and whose*.

Independent Clause   Dependent Clause

Example 1: This is the house ◄— **that** Jack built.

Independent Clause   Dependent Clause

Example 2: Is this the person ◄— **who** gave the most money?

Interrogative pronouns are specific words that are used to begin a question. There are five interrogative pronouns: *what, which, who, whom,* and *whose.*

> **Example 1: Which** man won the arm wrestling contest?
>
> **Example 2: Whose** flowers were used in that bouquet? Relative and Interrogative Pronouns

Practice 10: Relative and Interrogative Pronouns

Read the following sentences. Underline the relative or interrogative pronoun. Write R if one of the five pronouns described above is used as a relative pronoun. Write I if the pronoun is used as an interrogative pronoun. Write N if there are no relative or interrogative pronouns in the sentence.

1. April and Rene could not decide which task was more important. _____

2. To whom should I address this letter? _____

3. Which parents took all the kids to the circus? _____

4. There are many who believe that the pyramids were constructed by aliens. _____

5. Which of us will play goalie when we start the soccer game? _____

6. If Sheila and Patricia spend the day looking for Eric, what will Mary do? _____

7. Begging your pardon, why did you just dump your food on me? _____

8. This work seems to be a little risky. Which area is most dangerous? _____

9. Being angry is not an acceptable reason for any misbehavior. _____

10. On what day can he leave for the basketball trip? _____

11. Has Jessica considered leaving for the trip to Santa Fe, New Mexico? _____

12. The team finally decided who would be their leader. _____

13. For the rest of the year, I will send money to my credit card company. _____

14. Where is Kathy going to school when she moves to Los Angeles? _____

15. For whatever reason, Brady decided to take a walk through the woods and plant a garden. _____

CHAPTER 2 REVIEW

Rewrite each sentence. Correct errors in pronoun usage as well as plural and possessive noun errors.

1. Terri and me are taking a hike while you go to the Joness' house.

    _____

2. The trainers best student was willing to fight whoever would enter the ring.

    _____

3. The stock car race'rs highest speed was made in his final lap.

_____

4. Kevin Campbells' best memory was his wedding day.

_____

5. A thiefs' favorite time to break into you's apartments is between 9 a.m. and 5 p.m.

_____

6. The carnivals' success was due to it's owner, Joyce Hammerstein.

_____

7. All the sheeps were ready to go to these shearers across town to get their wool cut.

_____

8. Us civilians elect the commander-in-chief, and him or her must make important military decisions.

_____

9. We could hear many singers voices at the music festival.

_____

10. Who is going to open the door for that child I am holding?

_____

11. You go to the flower shop, and the rest of we will go to the drug store.

_____

12. That deers' food supply was plentiful in the forest.

_____

13. Whomever wants this assignment can have it.

_____

14. The alumnus at my school are all coming back for a special anniversary.

_____

15. This point in the previous quarter should have gone to us team during the dispute.

_____

16. Tyrones cousin wants to see how well him can dance.

_____

17. I put me chessboard down on the table and set up the pieces.

_____

18. That day was so hot, this streets' heat could have fried an egg.

_____

19. In a months' time, him's investment's value doubled.

_____

20. This clematis' flowers are very beautiful in the summer.

_____

21. The child expected that their work would be put on the bulletin board.

_____

22. Dad brought home ice cream from the Farmers Dairy for Tim and I.

_____

23. All is well here at ours country home.

_____

24. Those students backpacks were left at the museum.

_____

25. How do you know Doug is the one that gave us Mona's money?

_____

Each of the following sentences has a faulty pronoun reference. Rewrite each sentence to make the meaning clear.

26. They said we have no school tomorrow.

_____

27. In the middle of the book, it gets very exciting.

_____

28. Mike told him he could be on the team next year.

_____

29. Take the toy off the shelf and fix it.

_____

30. The vet told her that the dog had broken her foot.

_____

CHAPTER 2 TEST

Read each sentence. Select the underlined word that is a noun.

1. The <u>latest</u> comic book <u>catalog</u> is <u>coming</u> by mail <u>in</u> three days.

    A. latest   B. catalog   C. coming   D. in

2. <u>Kelly's</u> worst <u>experience</u> started <u>when</u> she tried to fix <u>her</u> knee.

    A. Kelly's   B. experience   C. when   D. her

3. <u>While</u> Jeffrey guarded the door, <u>I</u> slipped <u>inside</u> and took pictures of the <u>evidence</u>.

    A. While   B. I   C. inside   D. evidence

4. Alice, <u>competing</u> for a spot on <u>the</u> track <u>team</u>, tripped her competitor in the <u>right</u> lane.

    A. competing   B. the   C. team   D. right

Select the correct word to complete the sentence.

5. Shirley runs the race faster than _____ .

    A. they   B. them   C. their   D. ours

6. He wants to join with _____ this year.

    A. us   B. ourselves   C. they   D. we

7. Currently, _____ builds new apartments with me.

    A. him   B. hisself   C. his   D. he

8. I told _____ to lose weight by dieting.

    A. their   B. themselves   C. them   D. there

Select the correct word to replace the <u>underlined</u> part of the sentence.

   Example: <u>Tori and I</u> ate a sack lunch = <u>We</u> ate a sack lunch.

9. <u>The cheetah's</u> running speed is the fastest in the world.

    A. Its   B. His   C. It's   D. Hers

10. <u>Jerry and Matt's</u> favorite radio station is 99.7 FM.

    A. They're   B. Their   C. There   D. Them

11. Come to the ski shop with <u>Kim and I</u>, so you won't be left alone.

    A. us   B. we   C. our   D. hour

12. <u>Sarah</u> is very good at playing the soprano saxophone.

    A.   Her   B.   She   C.   Hers   D.   Its

Select the section of the sentence which has the incorrectly spelled noun, based on the rules for plural and possessive nouns.

13.
    A.   Give me two minuts,   C.   will be finished.
    B.   and your haircut   D.   no mistakes

14.
    A.   "I really like   C.   said the young girl.
    B.   that candy's flavor,"   D.   no mistakes

15.
    A.   The mouses were very tired   C.   entire loaf of bread.
    B.   after they ate through the   D.   no mistakes

16.
    A.   The townspeople waited   C.   for the wolves' attack.
    B.   until after sunset   D.   no mistakes

Read the following sentences. Decide which demonstrative pronoun or adjective is appropriate.

17. _____ flowers in my arms came from my garden.
    A.   This   B.   That   C.   These   D.   Those

18. _____ calico cat that I have in my hat will now disappear.
    A.   This   B.   That   C.   These   D.   Those

19. I reached this side of the river by placing my feet on _____ rock over there.
    A.   This   B.   That   C.   These   D.   Those

20. You can have some of _____ strawberries over there in the basket.
    A.   This   B.   That   C.   These   D.   Those

Read the following sentences. Choose the correct indefinite or relative pronoun.

21. _____ of you has money to spend for lunch.
    A.   Some   B.   Most   C.   Several   D.   Each

22. Terrell is the one _____ helped the new student from India.
    A.   that   B.   who   C.   which   D.   whom

23. She told me that _____ danced at her brother's wedding.
    A.   none   B.   something   C.   everybody   D.   either

24. There were _____ jackets Kendra wanted to buy.
    A.   several   B.   much   C.   most   D.   none

25. The best position _____ Ali can play on our team is quarterback.
    A.   who   B.   whom   C.   whose   D.   which

Chapter 3
Verbs and Verbals

This chapter references conventions	
ELA 8C1b	analyzes and uses simple, compound, complex, and compound-complex sentences correctly, punctuates properly, and avoids fragments and run-ons
ELA8C1c	revises sentences by correcting misplaced and dangling modifers
ELA8C1d	revises sentences by correcting errors in usage
ELA8C1e	demonstrates appropriate comma and semicolon usage (compound, complex, and compound-complex sentences, split dialogue, and for clarity)
ELA8C1f	analyzes the structure of a sentence (basic sentence parts, noun-adjective-adverb clauses and phrases)
ELA8C1g	produces final drafts/presentations that demonstrate accurate spelling and the correct use of punctuation and capitalization
ELA8W1	Writing Domain

A **verb** is a word that expresses a physical or mental action. It is a necessary part of every sentence. Verbs define whether an event took place in the past, present, or future. There are three types of verbs to learn: **action verbs, linking verbs,** and **helping verbs**.

Action verb - tells what is occurring, has occurred, or will occur.

> **Example 1:** Sarah swung from the rope into the lake.
>
> In this example, **swung** explains what Sarah did.

> **Example 2:** Emma ran the Boston Marathon.
>
> In this example, **ran** explains what Emma did.

Action verbs are divided into two categories: **transitive** and **intransitive**. Transitive verbs are **always** followed by a direct object. Intransitive verbs are **not** followed by a direct object. Often, the **same** verb can be used as a transitive verb or an intransitive verb.

> **Example 1:** Evan hit the baseball out of the ballpark.
>
> In this sentence, the noun *baseball* receives the action of the verb, **hit**. This makes **hit** a transitive verb.

Example 2: The storm hit at 3:00 p.m. on Saturday.

In this sentence, there is no word receiving the action of the verb, **hit**.

This makes **hit** an intransitive verb.

Here is a list of commonly used action verbs, both transitive and intransitive:

believe	cry	follow	live	see	talk
buy	cut	give	look	sell	taste
break	dance	go	love	send	think
bring	die	have	make	shout	travel
call	do	hear	meet	sing	turn
carry	drink	hit	need	sit	walk
clean	drive	hold	read	smell	want
climb	eat	jump	receive	smile	wash
cook	feel	know	ride	stand	wear
come	fight	laugh	run	swim	work
cost	fly	like	say	take	write

A **linking verb** is used to describe the subject by linking it to a word at or near the end of the sentence. This verb connects the subject with the predicate noun or adjective that describes it. In some cases, the linking verb simply states that the subject exists. These type of linking verbs are called **state-of-being verbs**.

Here is a list of some common linking verbs:

am	was	be	will be	feel	look
is	were	being	appear	grow	remain
are	became	been	become	get	act
seem	smell	sound	taste	stay	got

Example 1: The soup **tastes** great.

In this sentence, **tastes** is a word linking the subject, **soup**, to the adjective, **great**.

NOTE: In some cases, the same word used as a linking verb could also be an action verb in a different sentence. See example 2.

Example 2: The boy **tastes** the food carefully before eating.

Using the same verb as in example 1, **tastes**, we see that the boy is performing the **action** of tasting.

Example 3: The helicopter **is** on the launch pad.

In this sentence, the verb **is** tells the reader that the helicopter exists (state of being verb).

A **predicate noun** is a noun that comes after a linking verb. This noun is the same person or thing as the subject. In the example below, Dr. Willis and the veterinarian are the same person.

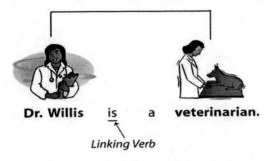

Dr. Willis is a **veterinarian.**

Linking Verb

In this example, **is** connects the subject, **Dr. Willis,** to a noun in the predicate, **veterinarian.**

A **predicate adjective** is an adjective that comes after a linking verb. This adjective describes something about the subject.

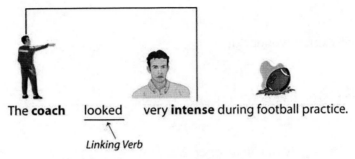

The **coach** looked very **intense** during football practice.

Linking Verb

Practice 1: Linking Verbs

Read the following sentences. Underline the linking verb. Draw a line connecting the subject to the predicate noun or adjective. Write PN for predicate noun and PA for predicate adjective in the blank after each sentence.

Example: Jessie Sharp <u>became</u> a judge after her law career was over. <u>PN</u>

1. The cheerleader seemed very cheerful at the Friday night basketball game. _____

2. Given more opportunities, Felix could have become a great dentist. _____

3. For two generations, the Boruchi tribe members were expert basket weavers. _____

4. The mood ring Cassadra wore turned green when she started laughing. _____

5. The compound remained stable until water was added. _____

6. Barry Rizzo became a rock star in a one-act play called, "Upon the Stage." _____

7. Although they had the flu, the athletes seemed healthy. _____

8. Because she did not rehearse the song, Kathy will be nervous. _____

9. By playing any song in reverse order, Ricky became a well-known keyboardist. _____

10. "That water looks very murky," Tyra said. _____

11. The barbecue ribs smell wonderful. _____

12. The bread in the plastic bag grew moldy in two days. _____

13. That man over there is my music teacher, Mr. Wigley. _____

14. "Your ideas sound great to me," said Charles. _____

15. Kate appeared exhausted after the four mile run. _____

Helping verb - a word or words that are added directly before another verb to make a verb phrase.

> **Example:** You **could have** fixed the car yourself!
> This sentence has two helping verbs, **could** and **have**.

> **Example:** Ted **has eaten** all the tomatoes.
> This sentence has one helping verb, **has.**

Here is a list of commonly used helping verbs:

do	has	could	can	will	am	was	being
does	have	should	may	shall	is	were	been
did	had	would	must	might	are	be	

Practice 2: Verbs

Read the following sentences. In the blanks provided, write A if the underlined word is an action verb, L if it is a linking verb, H if it is a helping verb, and N if the underlined word is not a verb.

Example: The little girl <u>feels</u> happy every time she has a slumber party.   L

1. Matt Damon's performance <u>was</u> spectacular. _____

2. The "Backstreet Boys" will be touring in <u>November</u>. _____

3. Given the chance, the PTA would <u>reelect</u> Patti Zuniga as their chairperson. _____

4. "<u>Tell</u> Darrell that I will bring back his basketball tomorrow," Janice said. _____

5. The tennis team players <u>have</u> used a new strategy to win their games. _____

6. In our restaurant, each table <u>is</u> shiny and sturdy. _____

7. Take her right hand, and <u>ask</u> her to dance with you. _____

8. The gray hummingbird <u>can</u> beat its wings over seventy times per second. _____

9. Jefferson Davis <u>was</u> president of the Confederacy during the Civil War. _____

10. Several folktales of the Southeast <u>are</u> preserved in a book called *Uncle Remus and His Friends*. _____

11. Luther and his brother Phil were <u>pulling</u> the rope to sound the bells. _____

12. The dinner rolls <u>taste</u> great after they have been lathered in hot butter. _____

13. <u>Dancing</u> is considered a high art form in many cultures. _____

14. Many people say that necessity <u>is</u> the mother of invention. _____

15. Climbing a steep, rugged mountain can <u>be</u> wonderful in the winter. _____

IDENTIFYING CORRECT VERB TENSES IN SENTENCES

The surrounding words in a sentence will dictate which **tense** a verb should take. Using various verbs, let's review the most commonly used **tenses** and **participles.**

1. **Present Tense** – used to express action or connection occurring **now, always, or repeatedly**.

   Example 1: We **work** in the produce department.
   Example 2: We **are** part of the team.

2. **Past Tense** – used to express a previous action or connection.
   Example 1: He **worked** at the fitness center yesterday.
   Example 2: You **were** there when he checked the belts.

3. **Future Tense** – indicates action that will begin at a later time.

> **Example 1:** Brian O'Donnell **will take** a trip to Mexico next year.

> **Example 2:** Courtney **will cut** Greg's hair next.

4. **Present Perfect** – used when a writer wants to describe one of two things:

1. An event that began in the past and was finished in the past.

2. An event that began in the past and continues to the present.

The present perfect tense is formed by combining the present tense of *to have* with a past participle verb. For example, *have walked, has spoken, has made, etc.*

> **Example 1:** The hungry crocodile **has eaten** the rabbit.   **Begins: Past   Ends: Past**
> > (ended action)

> **Example 2:** Dave **has worn** a cast for five months. **Begins: Past   Ends: Present**
> > (continuous action)

5. **Past Perfect** - this form is used when two events, both happening in the past, are discussed in time order. The past perfect tense is formed by combining the past tense form of *to have* with a past participle verb. For example, *had spoken, had read, had met, etc.*

> **Example 1:** By the time class ended, Jamal **had recited** part of the poem for his teacher.
> > In this example, Jamal had recited part of the poem **before** the class was over.

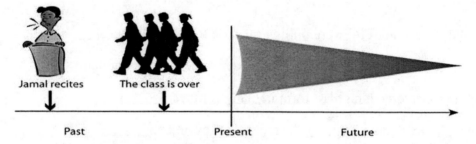

> **Example 2:** By the time she graduated from high school, Erin **had lived** in eight states.
> > In this example, one event that occurred continuously (Erin's moving) happened before another past event (Erin's graduation).

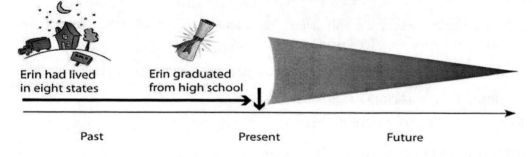

6. **Present Participle** - used when a writer wants to point out an action that is continuous, was continuous, or will be continuous or in progress. The present participle is formed by adding *-ing* to a verb.

> **Example 1:** **has been continuous** - I **was being** my usual self at the party.

> **Example 2:** **is continuous** - He **is studying** for his medical exam.

> **Example 3:** **will be continuous** - She **will be working** as a nurse.

7. **Past Participle** - used when an action has been completed. Some form of *be* or *have* must be used with a past participle to form a complete verb in a sentence.

> **Example 1:** DaVinci **had worked** hard on the *Mona Lisa*.

> **Example 2:** I **have been** at this school for two years.

8. **Future Perfect Tense** - signifies ongoing actions that will be finished by or before some specified time in the future.

> **Example 1:** In two weeks, the train shipment **will have arrived.**

> **Example 2:** If she becomes president of the United States, all their work **will have been** worth it.

VERB FORMS

On the following pages are two lists of some common forms of verbs. The first list contains **regular verbs**. The second list contains **irregular verbs**. Review these lists, and learn the verb forms you do not know. Then, remember these verbs to help you complete Practice 3.

REGULAR VERB FORMS

Verb	Singular Form	Plural Form	Past Tense	Present Participle	Past Participle
amaze	amazes	amaze	amazed	amazing	amazed
ask	asks	ask	asked	asking	asked
call	calls	call	called	calling	called
crash	crashes	crash	crashed	crashing	crashed
dance	dances	dance	danced	dancing	danced
fry	fries	fry	fried	frying	fried
honor	honors	honor	honored	honoring	honored
jog	jogs	jog	jogged	jogging	jogged
jump	jumps	jump	jumped	jumping	jumped
kill	kills	kill	killed	killing	killed
live	lives	live	lived	living	lived
love	loves	love	loved	loving	loved
pass	passes	pass	passed	passing	passed
plan	plans	plan	planned	planning	planned
receive	receives	receive	received	receiving	received
say	says	say	said	saying	said
seem	seems	seem	seemed	seeming	seemed
stare	stares	stare	stared	staring	stared
talk	talks	talk	talked	talking	talked
want	wants	want	wanted	wanting	wanted
wash	washes	wash	washed	washing	washed
work	works	work	worked	working	worked

IRREGULAR VERB FORMS

Verb	3rd Person Singular Form	Plural Form	Past Tense	Present Participle	Past Participle
be	is	are	was / were	being	been
burst	bursts	burst	burst	bursting	burst
choose	chooses	choose	chose	choosing	chosen
do	does	do	did	doing	done
draw	draws	draw	drew	drawing	drawn
eat	eats	eat	ate	eating	eaten
feel	feels	feel	felt	feeling	felt
fly	flies	fly	flew	flying	flown
give	gives	give	gave	giving	given
go	goes	go	went	going	gone
hear	hears	hear	heard	hearing	heard
know	knows	know	knew	knowing	known
leave	leaves	leave	left	leaving	left
make	makes	make	make	making	made
pay	pays	pay	paid	paying	paid
read	reads	read	read	reading	read
run	runs	run	ran	running	run
say	says	say	said	saying	said
see	sees	see	saw	seeing	seen
sing	sings	sing	sang	singing	sung
speak	speaks	speak	spoke	speaking	spoken
swim	swims	swim	swam	swimming	swum
take	takes	take	took	taking	taken
teach	teaches	teach	taught	teaching	taught
think	thinks	think	thought	thinking	thought
write	writes	write	wrote	writing	written

NOTE: The past participle of **freeze** is not **had freezed.** It is **had frozen.** The past tense of **sit** is not **sitted.** It is **sat.**

Practice 3: Verb Forms

Read the following sentences. Decide how each boldfaced verb should be changed, and then rewrite the sentence. **Note:** There may be more than one way to answer.

1. We played for three hours after Sharon **sings**.

   _____

2. Before returning to the hospital, the ambulance **arrive** at the scene of the accident.

   _____

3. She **stares** at the man in the double-breasted suit when he approached her.

   _____

4. You will return to school when you **felt** better.

   _____

5. After the dry cleaning, the suit **has looked** as good as new.

   _____

6. They **are washing** the dishes when the dishwasher broke down.

   _____

7. You **draw** well at the competition this year!

   _____

8. The senator **was taking** a trip across the state if he wins the election.

   _____

9. He and Crystal **have sailed** the boat in last year's competition.

   _____

10. The commercial pilot **had fly** over two hundred times in his career.

    _____

11. As the airplane approached the landing, we **will be** playing checkers.

    _____

12. Kendra's teacher told her that she **has been** a great doctor some day.

    _____

13. Troy **will play** baseball for six years before he moved away.

    _____

14. Chattanooga, Tennessee, **has been** an important railroad center during the Civil War.

_____

15. Thor **will always be staring** out the window when he was in grade school.

_____

16. When Dr. Kurtz stood in the auditorium, she **speaked** about the dangers of smoking.

_____

17. Since Tara **had been writing** a good essay, she was admitted to UCLA.

_____

18. Nate carries the school flag to every event because he **be** the class president.

_____

19. Janice Jordan, a professional storyteller, kept speaking as the boy **will make** a paper hat.

_____

20. Naomi told the children, "You **play** well yesterday!"

_____

COMMONLY CONFUSED VERBS

LIE   and   **LAY**

The verb **lie** means to rest or recline.   The verb **lay** means to place or put something down.

> **Example:** He enjoys **lying** in his hammock.
> The football player is **laying** the football in the grass.

	Present Tense	Past Tense	Past Participle
lie:	lie	lay	lain
lay:	lay	laid	laid

Practice 4: Lie and Lay

Read the following sentences. Fill in the blanks with the appropriate form of *lie* or *lay*.

1. Shauntee spent the summer day _____ in the sand at the beach.

2. Mr. Strickland is going to _____ down the rules when he comes to our school on Monday.

3. The mason _____ the bricks very carefully as he made the wall.

4. Miss Fran Thomaston _____ in the shade after working in her garden.

5. You had better _____ down now because you have a high fever.

6. Fluffy was _____ to rest at the Elm Street Pet Cemetery last Tuesday.

7. The students had to _____ their pencils on the desk when they were finished with the test.

8. You have _____ in bed for three days now! I am taking you outside for some sunshine.

9. The meteorite landed in the water and _____ there for thousands of years.

10. Uncle Joey _____ the baby back in the crib after she spit on him.

SIT   **and**   **SET**

The verb **sit** means to recline or rest.   The verb **set** means to place or put.

> **Example:** A man **sits** while ordering a meal.
> The golfer **sets** the ball on the tee.

	Past Tense	Past Tense	Past Participle
sit:	sit	sat	sat
set:	set	set	set

Practice 5: Sit and Set

Read the following sentences. Fill in the blanks with the appropriate form of *sit* or *set*.

1. We _____ the orange cones out to redirect traffic.

2. They had_____ in the same reclining chairs during this whole episode of *Friends*.

3. The children _____ the dining room table for eight.

4. During the performance, we _____ and watched the symphony play.

5. Chuck came over to my house to play the game system while _____ on my sofa.

6. The milk _____ out for three days and turned sour.

7. We used a clamp so we could _____ the table leg in place.

8. After her workout, she usually _____ the jump rope on the ground.

9. The elderly couple _____ together on the plane.

10. The reader _____ the books on the front counter of the library.

11. You _____ the mood by opening the windows and allowing the sunlight to enter the room.

12. "If I have to _____ and wait for another minute, I'm going to lose it!" the anxious father-to-be said.

CAN, SHALL, and WILL   *Versus*   COULD, SHOULD, and WOULD

The verb forms of *can, shall,* and *will* are used to indicate the **future** tense. The verb forms of *could, should,* and *would* are used to indicate the **conditional** tense.

Conditional Verbs - verbs that have some uncertainty or doubt about the future associated with them.

The verb **should** indicates obligation. The verbs **could** and **would** are used in polite requests. The verb **can** indicates the ability to do something. The verbs **shall** and **will** are used when there is no doubt as to what is going to happen in the future.

> **Example 1:** If you know for a fact you are going to the blues concert, say: "I **will** (**shall**) go to the blues concert."

> **Example 2:** If you are unsure if you ought to go to the blues concert, say: "**Should** I go to the blues concert?"

> **Example 3:** If you want to politely request something such as cake, say: "**Could** (**Would**) you bring me some cake?"

> **Example 4:** If you think you are able to bring someone a piece of cake, say: "I **can** bring you a piece of cake."

Practice 6: Can, Shall, Will / Could, Should, Would

Read the following sentences. Fill in the blanks with one of the six verbs discussed: *can, shall, will, could, should, would*

1. _____ you please bring me a warm blanket? (conditional-polite request)

2. What do you think I _____ do in this situation? (conditional - unsure)

3. She _____ give you her most beautiful dress if you ask her nicely. (future)

4. The Department of Transportation _____ give you what you need. (ability - future)

5. Since we have the time, we _____ help that lady fix her yard. (conditional - obligation)

6. _____ I bring the kids to the table now? (future)

7. What _____ he do if the car loan does not go through? (ability - future)

8. The teacher said, "Jimmy, _____ you please come to my desk?" (conditional - polite)

9. Sade _____ be taking the 9:00 a.m. bus to Chicago. (future)

10. Do you think Gail _____ take the job or not? (conditional - obligation)

VERBALS

There are three kinds of verbals: **gerunds**, **infinitives**, and **participles**.

GERUNDS

A **gerund** is a verb ending in *-ing* that functions as a noun. Gerunds may become subjects or objects in a sentence.

As a subject: Wasting cardboard is bad for the environment. In this example, **Wasting** is the gerund because it is a verb ending in *-ing* and is also acting as the subject of the sentence.

As an object: She escaped her daily routine by reading. In this example, **reading** is the gerund because it is a verb ending in *-ing* that is also the object of the preposition *by*.

Practice 7: Gerunds

Read the following sentences. First, underline the verbs. Then place parentheses around the gerund, a verb ending in -ing that is acting as a noun. Some sentences do not contain gerunds.

Example 1: The sprinter is racing toward the goal.
In this example, *racing* is not in parentheses because it is acting as a verb, describing the sprinter's action, not as a noun.

Example 2: (Bowling) is one of my favorite activities.
In this example, *bowling* is a gerund. It is also the subject of the sentence.

1. One of her greatest fears is driving in a thunderstorm.

2. The volleyball was sailing through the air between the hometown team and the visitors.

3. The clown was losing his balance after stepping on a banana peel.

4. Selling requires a great deal of charisma and determination.

5. The teeth of any animal are very important for chewing.

6. Several of our scouts are watching the players closely.

7. Speaking a foreign language has helped you get better jobs here.

8. By studying his opponent, Jason was able to gain many advantages.

9. Misty and her friends went skating for four hours.

10. Smoking is prohibited in public buildings.

11. Scratches on the coffee table are increasing quickly thanks to the children.

12. Relaxing in a hot bath is a great way to relieve stress.

13. Jake enjoys spending time with his family on vacation.

14. David Penna was racing his bike and went crashing through the barrier.

15. How much did you earn for running the homeless shelter?

INFINITIVES

An **infinitive** is formed by placing the word **to** in front of the base form of a verb. The infinitive can be used in a sentence as a noun, adjective, or adverb. Because of its versatility, the infinitive is often needed when constructing sentences.

You will need to ask yourself what the *purpose* of the infinitive is in each sentence in order to distinguish it as a noun, an adjective, or an adverb.

As a noun:	I need **to time** the cooking of the meat for exactly thirty minutes.
	In this sentence, the infinitive **to time** is used as the object of the sentence. Usually, infinitives are **not** used as subjects of sentences.
As an adjective:	She needed a house **to call** her own.
	In this sentence, the infinitive **to call** is an adjective describing the noun, **house.**
As an adverb:	The guest showed his cards **to prove** he wasn't cheating.
	In this sentence the infinitive **to prove** acts as an adverb by answering the question, "Why did he show his cards?" Thus, the infinitive acts as an adverb modifying the verb, **showed.**

Practice 8: Infinitives

Read the following sentences. Place parentheses around the infinitives. To the right side write N if the infinitive acts as a noun, Adj. if it acts as an adjective, or Adv. if it acts as an adverb.

> **Example:** The boy had enough sense (**to go**) to the police.   *-Adj.*

1. You had better file your tax return if you want to stay out of trouble.

2. Follow me upstairs if you need to rest from your journey.

3. The new student was looking for someone to study with over lunch.

4. The club members had to agree to a unanimous decision.

5. George Golding needs a new glove to play baseball.

6. The band gave a longer concert to surprise their fans.

7. Shannon knew to have a camcorder was a big expense.

8. Shamie spent her allowance to buy the most expensive kitty litter for her new kitten.

9. Peter sent us to get a room at our destination.

10. To remember what we read requires careful note-taking.

PARTICIPLES

Participle - a word that is formed from a verb but is used as an adjective.

There are four different kinds of participles: **past participle**, **present participle**, **perfect participle**, and **passive participle**.

Past participle - to make a verb into a past participle, simply add **-en** or **-ed** to the base form of the verb or use a special spelling for irregular verbs. For example: eat = eaten, starve = starved, bleed = bled, read = read.

> **Example:** The **sunken** living room looks great in your house.
> Here, the word **sunken** acts as an adjective describing **living room**.

Present participle - to make a verb into a present participle, add **-ing** to the verb.
For example: skate = skating, fly = flying, drive = driving.

> **Example:** **Growing** restless, the travelers left the airport.
> Here, the word **growing** acts as an adjective describing the noun, **travelers**.

Perfect participle - to make a verb into a perfect participle, place the word **having** in front of the past participle form of the verb. For example: say = having said, yell = having yelled, crawl = having crawled.

> **Example:** **Having flown** to Paris, Billy felt lost because he couldn't speak French.
> Here, the words **having flown** act as an adjective modifying **Billy**.

Passive participle - to make a verb into a passive participle, place the word **having been** in front of the past participle form of the verb. For example, make = having been made, solve = having been solved, write = having been written.

> **Example:** **Having been carved** out of onyx, the statues were shiny and smooth.
> Here, the words **having been carved** act as an adjective modifying **statues.**

Practice 9: Participles

Read the sentences below. Place parentheses around the participles, and underline the nouns they modify.

> **Example:** The (driving) <u>force</u> on this team has been the quarterback, Mitch Malcolm.

1. Having dropped out of an airplane, Daffy Duck landed on a bale of straw.

2. My physical education teacher, Ms. Nguyen, made us exercise on inflated mattresses.

3. The dancing puppet made me laugh until my stomach hurt.

4. Having been awarded a Nobel prize, the physicist became instantly famous.

5. For many years, the three of us knew the talking horse, Mr. Ed.

6. The termites, having feasted on the old house, moved on to the newly-built subdivision.

7. Having been given recess for an hour, the children played hide-and-seek.

8. When we saw David Copperfield's death-defying performance, we gasped in terror.

9. The woman pulled out her yellowing wedding dress and remembered her special day.

10. Our drama instructor showed us the painted landscapes we would be using.

CHAPTER 3 REVIEW

Read the following sentences. Underline the verb in each sentence. Then, place the verbals in parentheses. On the blank line, tell whether the verbal is a gerund, infinitive, or participle.

> **Example:** (Swimming) <u>is</u> my favorite sport. <u>Gerund</u>   Is is underlined because it is the verb.
> **Swimming** is in parentheses because it is a verbal. Swimming is also a gerund because it acts as a noun.

1. Theona loved to take naps after lunch. _____

2. The new fifty dollar bills circulating later this year should be very popular. _____

3. Given the opportunity, Greg will probably take the frozen food given to him. _____

4. To avoid starvation, Maurissa ate all the berries she could. _____

5. Storing the medicine correctly will ensure the baby's safety. _____

6. Staring is considered inappropriate in many cultures. _____

7. All your body's movements are controlled by contracting and expanding specific groups of muscles. _____

Read the following sentences. Decide how each boldfaced verb should be changed, then rewrite the sentence.

8. Before the third day of practice is finished, Erica Ginsburg **had been** playing three different *arpeggios*.

_____

9. Can you **wrote** down the notes for me in class? _____

_____

10. Graham **be** talking in class even when it's not his turn. _____

_____

11. By the time she found the camera, the gorilla **disappeared**. _____

_____

12. Big Ben **will fight** Godzilla bravely on television last night. _____

_____

Read the following sentences. In the blanks provided, write A if the boldfaced word is an action verb, L if it is a linking verb, and H if it is a helping verb.

13. Luke **remained** seated until it was his turn to be called. _____

14. Larry **had** opened the door for the elderly woman. _____

15. The whole team **is** going to eat pizza tonight. _____

16. Those cowboys **ride** their horses daily. _____

17. Our tomato plants **grow** bigger and faster each year. _____

Read the sentences below. Circle the correct form of the verb.

18. They had (set / sat) the ripe orange on the table.

19. The surgeon asked the nurse, "(Should / Could) you hand me the scalpel?"

20. The doctor told you to (lie / lay) in bed for the next two weeks.

21. Sarah (will / can) {*ability*} bring you a delicious piece of honey chicken if you ask her nicely.

22. Floyd (set / sat) in the rocking chair with his new kitten, Spacey.

CHAPTER 3 TEST

Choose the correct subject or verb in the following sentences.

1. The _____ burns when you leave it in the microwave too long.

   A. kernels   B. popcorn   C. cinnamon rolls   D. pizza snacks

2. Once the building is remodeled, the tenants _____ moving in.

   A. are   B. has been   C. is   D. was

3. We _____ clothes whenever it's time to leave school.

   A. changes   C. is changing

   B. has been changing   D. change

4. _____ has prepared you to take tests.

   A. We   B. I   C. Studying   D. Your teachers

5. Be sure you _____ two pounds of bananas when you go to the store.

   A. buys   B. has bought   C. buy   D. is buying

6. _____ are singing every Friday in our civic center.

   A. Entertainers   C. A comedian

   B. Willie Nelson   D. A crowd

7. Skydiving is deadly when _____ forget their parachutes.

   A. the leader   B. Alex   C. the skydivers   D. she

8. The electrical wiring _____ in the kitchen and the living room.

   A. Are being installed   C. have been installed

   B. were installed   D. is being installed

9. _____ the emergency button now!

   A. Presses   B. Press   C. Have pressed   D. Pressing

10. _____ gives Jenny a flower every Saturday.

   A. You   B. The soccer players   C. Jeff   D. The band members

Read the following sentences. Identify whether the word underlined is a verb, gerund, infinitive, or participle.

11. Steve is <u>gaining</u> weight for the next football game.

   A. verb   B. infinitive   C. gerund   D. participle

12. We threw away the <u>uncooked</u> hamburger because it had been out too long.

   A. verb   B. infinitive   C. gerund   D. participle

13. Richie needed the ball <u>to play</u> a game of roller hockey.

   A. verb   B. infinitive   C. gerund   D. participle

14. Cynthia loved <u>making</u> paper dolls for the children's hospital.
    A. verb   B. infinitive   C. gerund   D. participle

15. Ryan and my little brother, Jed, like to play with Mexican <u>jumping</u> beans.
    A. verb   B. infinitive   C. gerund   D. participle

16. <u>Belching</u> is considered a compliment after a meal in Mongolia.
    A. verb   B. infinitive   C. gerund   D. participle

17. "Feel free <u>to make</u> yourself useful in the kitchen," Mom said.
    A. verb   B. infinitive   C. gerund   D. participle

18. The tightrope, having been <u>taken</u> for repairs, was not available for the first performance.
    A. verb   B. infinitive   C. gerund   D. participle

Read the following sentences. Identify the correct form of the verb below.

19. Can you please _____ still while I take your temperature?
    A. sit   B. sat   C. set   D. none of the above

20. If you _____ under that tree for a second, I'll go bring us some food.
    A. lay   B. lie   C. laid   D. lain

21. If I see someone stranded by the side of the road, I _____ (obligation) find a way to help him or her.
    A. could   B. should   C. can   D. will

22. The three men _____ a world record in the relay race.
    A. sit   B. sat   C. set   D. seated

23. Isabel _____ (future) purchase the convertible as soon as she has the money.
    A. could   B. should   C. can   D. will

Read the following sentences. Select the correct verb form for the boldfaced word.

24. The bus driver always **looks** mad when the kids don't stay in their seats.
    A. helping verb   B. linking verb   C. action verb   D. not a verb

25. Our chess team **meets** on Thursdays at 4:00 p.m.
    A. helping verb   B. linking verb   C. action verb   D. not a verb

26. The prom king wore the **painted** robe.
    A. helping verb   B. linking verb   C. action verb   D. not a verb

27. The elderly man **had been** saving for this trip around the world for his entire life.
    A. helping verb   B. linking verb   C. action verb   D. not a verb

28. The illusionist **seems** happy when he is performing.
    A. action verb   B. linking verb   C. action verb   D. not a verb

Chapter 4
Sentences/Subject-Verb Agreement

This chapter references conventions	
ELA 8C1b	analyzes and uses simple, compound, complex, and compound-complex sentences correctly, punctuates properly, and avoids fragments and run-ons
ELA8C1c	revises sentences by correcting misplaced and dangling modifers
ELA8C1d	revises sentences by correcting errors in usage
ELA8C1f	analyzes the structure of a sentence (basic sentence parts, noun-adjective-adverb clauses and phrases)

Simple Subjects and Simple Predicates

A sentence must contain a simple subject and a simple predicate.

Rule 1.   **A simple subject is a word or group of words that tells what the sentence is about.**

Rule 2.   **The simple predicate is a verb or group of verbs that asks or says something about the subject or tells what the subject is doing.**

In the following examples, the simple subject is in parentheses, and the simple predicate is underlined.

Example 1: (Flipper), the movie star dolphin, <u>swam</u> in the ocean.

Example 2: (Life) <u>is</u> but a dream.

Example 3: (Carol) and (Julie) <u>are hiking</u> in the Appalachian Mountains.

In Example 3, when two or more subjects perform the same action, the verb tense becomes plural **(are hiking,** not **is hiking).**

Sentences that are questions must be turned into a statement to determine the simple **subject and predicate**

Example 4: Do you want to jump off this rock?

Rearranged (You)   <u>do want</u> to jump off this rock.

        Simple Subject   Simple Predicate

Verb phrases that include two or more words, such as <u>is lying</u> in Example 5, are often split apart when asking a question.

Example 5: Why <u>is</u> the (cat) <u>lying</u> on the new carpet?

Practice 1: Simple Subjects and Simple Predicates

In the following sentences, put parentheses around the simple subject, and underline the simple predicate.

Example: (I) <u>am learning</u> Spanish this year.

1. The five tigers have been eating more than usual.

2. My friend's dog is going to bite her if he escapes.

3. The white flour sold in stores has been bleached.

4. Tyrannosaurus Rex was a vicious dinosaur.

5. Carrie and Lynn took the motorcycle back to the store.

6. Garfield, the cat, loves to eat lasagna.

7. How many stories like that have you told?

8. For goodness sake, how did you get into a fight?

9. Our friend, Lisa, is taking a trip to Europe with her class.

10. Paul is on his way to meet Cain at the bookstore.

11. All of the ships were sailing to Colombia.

12. Seedless watermelon grows quickly in the summer months.

13. How many stars are in the universe?

14. Professor Sawyer combined the elements chlorine and sodium in a beaker.

15. The gifts given at Christmas were very inexpensive.

16. Are you looking for Chris?

17. Too much food is bad for the stomach

18. Many teens enjoy hanging out in the malls after school.

19. Too much work and not enough play make for a tiring day.

20. Many students speak Spanish in California, Florida, and Texas.

PHRASES AND CLAUSES

A **phrase** is a group of words acting together as a unit. For example, the participial phrase **arriving very late** consists of three words that together are considered as part of the participle, **arriving**. Phrases are not complete sentences but are parts of sentences.

> **Example:** Everyone wanted to see clearly.
> In this sentence, **to see clearly** is the infinitive phrase. The word **clearly** modifies the infinitive **to see**. These three words together make an infinitive phrase.

A **clause** is an arrangement of words containing a subject and a predicate that can be **part** of a sentence. A clause can also be a sentence by itself.

An **independent clause** is a group of words that could stand alone as a sentence. However, the clause may be grouped with other clauses or phrases.

> **Example:** We asked to see Vicki after the show was over.
> In this sentence, the independent clause is **We asked to see Vicki.** The first five words of the sentence could stand alone as a simple sentence. **We** is the subject and **asked** is the verb.

A **dependent clause** is a group of words that cannot stand alone as a sentence, yet it contains a subject and a verb. A dependent clause is connected to the entire sentence by a **relative pronoun** or by a **subordinating conjunction**.

> **Example:** Swimming is more enjoyable when the water is warm.
> In this sentence, **when the water is warm** is the dependent clause. The last five words of this sentence contain both a subject, **water**, and a verb, **is**.

A **relative pronoun** or a **subordinating conjunction** will introduce a dependent clause. Study these lists of **relative pronouns** and **subordinating conjunctions**:

Relative Pronouns		Subordinating Conjunctions			
who	which	after	before	unless	while
whose	that	although	if	until	why
whom		as	since	when	
		because	though	where	

> **Example 1:** Because they drove all night, they arrived in San Antonio at dawn.
> In this sentence, the independent clause is **they arrived in San Antonio at dawn**. This part of the sentence could stand alone. **They** is the subject, and **arrived** is the verb. **Because they drove all night** is the dependent clause. The subordinating conjunction, **because**, introduces the dependent clause.

> **Example 2:** Anton has a video game that is very challenging.
> In this sentence, **that is very challenging** is the dependent clause. The relative pronoun, **that**, refers to the subject, **video game**, and <u>is</u> becomes the verb. **Anton has a video game** is the independent clause.

Practice 2: Types of Sentences

Read the following sentences. Write P if the bolded words make a phrase. Write I if the bolded words make an independent clause. Write D if the bolded words make a dependent clause.

Example: The three children took the stroller **around the corner**. ___P___

1. The team **that everyone thought would lose** won the game. _____

2. **Daniel told a frightening ghost story** after playing Capture the Flag. _____

3. Our team surprised us all by scoring a goal **during the last minute**. _____

4. The carpenter started the house **by measuring carefully**. _____

5. **Ms. Stanton left her position** after learning of her company's unlawful practices. _____

6. Becky bought the diapers **two days after she had her baby**. _____

7. Mr. Mendoza climbed the cliff **with the help of his comrades**. _____

8. Our soccer team did a great deal of fundraising **to aid autistic children**. _____

9. You should never spend money **that you do not have**. _____

10. **If the story is true**, we are all going to be in the papers. _____

11. Hold my hand **while we walk across the stream**. _____

12. I saw an exciting movie **at the dollar theater**. _____

13. When the dog started barking, **the stranger left the neighborhood**. _____

14. *Call of the Wild* is one of Mary Fran's favorite books. _____

15. Hector replied, "**My teacher told me** why I got a 60 on my test." _____

16. **Before he moved to Miami**, Mr. Aikens gave me his new phone number. _____

17. Fabio is the student **whose father spoke to our class**. _____

18. Even though I take care of my brothers and sisters, I get **good grades in school**. _____

19. **Though some people speak English in Puerto Rico**, most people speak Spanish. _____

20. I was the one **who dressed like a clown** at my mom's surprise birthday party. _____

TYPES OF SENTENCES

Sentences are classified by structure in one of four ways: **simple, compound, complex,** and **compound-complex sentences**. In the examples below, independent clauses are underlined, and dependent clauses are kept in regular type.

A **simple sentence** is a sentence made of one independent clause. It may have more than one subject or more than one predicate. It may have phrases also.

> **Example 1:** Billy took the boys fishing after school.
>
> **Example 2:** Today was hot and dry.

A **compound sentence** is a sentence made of two or more simple sentences joined by a semicolon or a comma and the conjunctions *and, but, or, nor, for, so,* or *yet*. It can contain two or more independent clauses.

> **Example 1:** Gladis took the car to the mechanic, but she forgot to bring her checkbook.
>
> **Example 2:** We ate a large breakfast; then we skipped lunch.

A **complex sentence** is a sentence containing one independent clause and one or more dependent clauses. Relative pronouns or subordinating conjunctions are used to relate the sentences together.

> **Example 1:** Because of the smoke, the elderly man could not enter the building.
>
> **Example 2:** The car that she likes the best is a Lexus.

A **compound-complex sentence** is a sentence containing two or more compound sentences and one or more complex sentences.

> **Example 1:** When her mother planned Crystal's birthday party, she first made an invitation list, and then she planned the food menu and the cake design.
>
> **Example 2:** Before we buy shoes, my mom looks for bargains, but sometimes we splurge.

Here is a chart explaining the composition of all four types of complex sentences.

Type of Sentence	Number of Independent Clauses	Number of Dependent Clauses
simple	1	0
compound	2 or more	0
complex	1	1 or more
compound-complex	2 or more	1 or more

Practice 3: More Types of Sentences

Read the following sentences. In the blanks after each sentence, write S if the sentence is simple, Cd if the sentence is compound, Cx if the sentence is complex, and CC if the sentence is compound-complex.

1. Mary pruned the bushes while Ben mowed the lawn. _____

2. Dolores and Ricki went canoeing with their friends after church on Sunday. _____

3. Eve sewed her feather-filled coat to prepare for the onslaught of winter. _____

4. Three divers are trying out for a spot on the team, and there is only one dive remaining. _____

5. At 6:30 p.m., Phil Moore left his house; we have no record of him after that. _____

6. After his car hit the bridge and flipped over, Rodney needed to get to the doctor quickly, and his wife turned on her cellular phone and dialed 911. _____

7. Since Paul ran faster than all of his classmates, he won the prize. _____

8. I was late for school because I missed the school bus. _____

9. Never talk to strangers, and call 911 if you have an emergency. _____

10. They enjoy playing kickball during gym class. _____

11. After we finished dinner, we all went out to a movie, and we stopped at Brewster's for ice cream. _____

12. Natalie stayed up until 3 a.m. and still got up this morning to get to school. _____

13. She was only 20 years old when she graduated from college, her proud parents sitting in the front row. _____

14. The human body is very resilient, but when pushed to extremes for too long a period, it will let you know. _____

15. Antarctica would be the smallest continent if you counted only the actual land. _____

16. Jack and Cathy went to the store with their mother. _____

17. When the Pilgrims landed in November of 1620, they needed to find food and shelter if they were to survive. _____

18. Drunk drivers put more than their own lives in danger; they endanger everyone on the road. _____

19. It was cold and drafty in the second floor apartment. _____

20. Jamie and his go-cart came crashing through the barrier. _____

SUBJECT-VERB AGREEMENT

Grammar rules state that the *subject* of the sentence must agree with the corresponding *verb* of the sentence. The *subject* is the word performing the action (*verb*). In the examples below, each subject is underlined and each verb is in parentheses.

Example 1: My older brothers (play) baseball in the park.

Example 2: The frog (croaks) in the pond every night.

By reviewing the infinitive verb **to be**, you can see how the verb must agree with the subject. Following is the conjugation of **to be** in the present tense.

	Subject	Verb		Subject	Verb
1st person singular	I	am	**1st person plural**	we	are
2nd person singular	you	are	**2nd person plural**	you	are
3rd person singular	he, she, it	is	**3rd person plural**	they	are

The subject of the sentence does not have to appear before the verb to be the subject. (In questions and in sentences with *here* and *there*, the verb comes before the subject.)

Example 1: When is Dorothy coming to plant her flowers? In this example, **Dorothy** is the subject and dictates the agreement with the verb **is**.

Example 2: Here comes your special order of pizza. In this example, **order** is the subject, and **comes** is the verb.

NOTE: Some words having an **s** at the end are also singular subjects, for example, **news**, **physics**, **mathematics**, and so on.

Two or more subjects connected by *and* need a plural verb form.

Example 1: Jack and Jill are in the corner.

Example 2: Pizza, candy, and hamburgers are my favorite foods.

Sentences containing compound singular subjects have verbs that are written as **compound singular**.

Example 1: In addition to Keri, Rick is entered in the contest.
In Example 1, **Keri** and **Rick** are both subjects of this sentence. Because the sentence interrupter, **in addition to** is used, the verb **is entered** becomes singular.

Example 2: Either Susan or Allie walks down the aisle at the rehearsal.
In example 2, **Susan** and **Allie** are both subjects of this sentence. Because the sentence interrupter, **either...or** is used, the verb **walks** becomes singular.

When subjects are joined by *and* but considered as a unit or refer to one person or thing, then use a singular verb form.

> **Example 1:** Macaroni and cheese is my favorite dinner.

> **Example 2:** Her favorite aunt and her godmother was Mary Reagan.

When the word *each* or *every* comes before the subjects joined by *and*, use a singular verb.

> **Example 1:** Each man and woman is responsible for cleaning up.

> **Example 2:** Every boy and girl needs to bring markers tomorrow.

Practice 4: Subject - Verb Agreement

Read the following sentences. Write a C next to the sentence if the subject and the underlined present tense verb *agree*. Correct the verb in the present tense if it *does not agree* with the subject

1. Mickey Mouse <u>makes</u> funny comments during his cartoons.

2. Mrs. Nally and her friends <u>plays</u> cards during the night.

3. The new riding lawn mower <u>run</u> smoothly.

4. Now <u>is</u> the time to change the future.

5. Theresa <u>want</u> to be the class president.

6. There <u>is</u> five pencils on the floor.

7. Instead of steak, <u>eat</u> the shrimp.

8. The genie <u>grant</u> three wishes to the one who releases him.

9. I <u>smile</u> whenever I see a clown.

10. Louise and Rita <u>is</u> going to Disneyland.

11. Because of a death in the family, Jeff Ranier <u>is</u> not available for appointments.

12. Steve, in addition to Mike, <u>check</u> all the locks in the building every night.

13. Neither Nathan nor his brother <u>walk</u> to school.

14. We accountants <u>calculates</u> the taxes owed by various companies.

15. The congregation <u>rise</u> up singing when the preacher walks to the pulpit.

16. Ann, in addition to Steve, <u>are</u> present at the wedding ceremony.

17. Here <u>is</u> the peanuts you ordered.

18. A meteorite from Mars sometimes <u>fall</u> to the earth.

19. When <u>is</u> Megan and Madison coming in today?

20. There <u>go</u> your car down the hill with no one in it!

SUBJECT-VERB AGREEMENT WITH COLLECTIVE NOUNS

Collective nouns have special agreement problems. Collective nouns have either a singular meaning or a plural meaning. If the group acts together as one unit, the noun is singular and needs a singular verb. If the collective noun refers to the members of the group acting individually, the noun is plural and needs a plural verb.

> **Example 1:** The **committee** meets in the room down the hall.
> The committee is acting as one unit and reaches a decision, so we use the singular verb, **meets**.

> **Example 2:** The **committee** leave their homes at different times.
> Here the committee are acting as individuals, so we use the plural noun, **leave**.

Practice 5: More Subject - Verb Agreement

For each of the following sentences, first decide if the collective noun is acting as a unit or individuals. Then underline the correct verb.

1. My class cannot (agree, agrees) on where to go for a class picnic.

2. This class (is, are) very quiet today.

3. The orchestra (was, were) looking over their new music.

4. Our school orchestra (is, are) ranked first in the state.

5. The army (was, were) fighting for their lives during the conflict.

6. The army (use, uses) anyone who qualifies for the job.

7. The pack of wolves (live, lives) in a den.

8. The pack of wolves spread out and (surround, surrounds) their prey.

9. The crew (go, goes) to their homes for lunch.

10. The crew (depend, depends) on supplies being delivered on time to the job site.

11. The flock of ducks (scatter, scatters) when they hear the crack of a hunting rifle.

12. The flock of ducks (fly, flies) south for the winter.

13. The band (play, plays) at every football game.

14. The band must (sell, sells) fifty candy bars each to raise money for new instruments.

15. The audience (give, gives) a standing ovation when they like the performance.

16. The audience (is, are) leaving through the back doors.

17. The navy (is, are) required to be in their uniforms while they are on duty.

18. The navy (is, are) being sent to the South Pacific.

19. My team (was, were) encouraged to do their best at every football practice.

20. My team (is, are) going to win the game again this Friday!

MISPLACED MODIFIERS

A **modifier** is a phrase or clause that helps clarify the meaning of another word.

> **Example:** Tipping over the trash can, our cat was looking for food.

In this sentence, the phrase **Tipping over the trash can** modifies the word **cat**. Sometimes the meanings of entire sentences are confused when a modifier is not placed in the correct location in a sentence. These types of phrases and clauses are called **misplaced modifiers**.

As seen in the example above, a **modifying phrase** is a phrase that clarifies the meaning of a word. In some instances, modifying phrases can be misplaced in a sentence.

> **Example:** Two students competed against the school record diving in the swimming pool.

In this sentence, it is unclear whether the phrase **diving in the swimming pool** describes the students or the school record. To correct this problem, place the modifying phrase closer to the word it describes.

> **Corrected:** Diving in the swimming pool, two students competed against the school record.

A **modifying clause** is a dependent or independent clause that clarifies the meaning of another word.

> **Example:** Raymond waited for his test results pacing nervously on the steps.

In this sentence, it is unclear whether the clause **pacing nervously on the steps** describes **Raymond** or **test results**. To correct this problem, place the modifying clause closer to the word it describes.

> **Corrected:** Pacing nervously on the steps, Raymond waited for his test results.

Practice 6: Misplaced Modifiers

The following sentences contain misplaced modifiers. Rewrite each sentence correctly on the lines provided. Write C if the modifier is correctly placed in the sentence.

1. Grandpa Frank who was called Carlene brought a set of clothes for the baby girl.

   _____

2. Neal worked hard on his farm raising cattle to support his family.

   _____

3. The teacher announced that next week's class, which would encourage more participation, would be about international foods.

_____

_____

4. The travel agency is now providing added incentives for customers vacationing in October.

_____

5. One of our scouts sighted a tank through night vision glasses that he could not identify.

_____

6. The new Arts Center was funded by Mrs. Stanworth, who has since passed away, at a cost of $1,500,000.00.

_____

_____

7. The investigators reduced the number of banks that the criminals might attempt to rob to six.

_____

8. A careless person drove the large forklift through the narrow aisle without looking.

_____

9. Thrown recklessly last Tuesday, the children were forced to pay damages for breaking the neighbor's window with a baseball.

_____

_____

10. The dock allows people to enter and leave their houseboats who live on the river.

_____

DANGLING MODIFIERS

A **dangling modifier** is a phrase or clause that comes at the beginning of a sentence but does not modify (describe) the subject in the sentence.

    Example: Listening to hip hop music, her arms began to move with the rhythm.

In this example, the phrase **Listening to hip hop music** modifies the subject, **arms**, in this sentence. Since arms cannot listen to music, the phrase **Listening to hip hop music** cannot be the modifier of **arms**. Therefore, this phrase is a **dangling modifier**.

    Corrected: Listening to hip hop music, Latasha began to move her arms to the rhythm.

Listening to hip hop music correctly describes **Latasha** instead of **arms**.

Practice 7: Dangling Modifiers

Read the following sentences. Rewrite the sentences so that they no longer contain dangling modifiers. Write C if the modifier is used correctly.

1. While fishing in the river, a large piece of driftwood floated by.

   _____

2. Left penniless by the taxes, his hunger grew larger.

   _____

3. To decide a military action, the long-term outcome must be planned by the generals.

   _____

4. While flying high above the Rocky Mountains in the clouds, a flash of lightning hit the front of our plane.

   _____

   _____

5. Working in this beach side resort for several months, the lobsters were caught by many life-guards.

   _____

6. Taking control of the wheel when my father fell asleep, the street lights guided me to a stopping place.

   _____

   _____

7. While barely a teenager in middle school, my dog ate my homework.

   _____

8. After volunteering in the local hospital, her days were filled with a sense of happiness.

   _____

9. Before the space shuttle was scheduled to launch, a thunderstorm arose, causing postponement of the launch.

   _____

   _____

10. While planting trees in Seattle, her car remained in San Antonio.

    _____

CHAPTER 4 REVIEW

Read each of the following sentences. If the subjects and verbs disagree, rewrite the sentences. Then state whether the sentence is *simple, compound, complex,* or *compound-complex.*

Example: When the sun rose, we were working, and when the sun sets, we were sleeping.

Rewritten: When the sun rose, we were working, and when the sun set, we were sleeping.
compound-complex

1. Jan's keys was in her brother's wallet, and she could not start her car.

_____

2. In the past, Steve will not take piano lessons.

_____

3. By the time the rain stopped, we has finished doing our homework and cleaning every room in the house.

_____

_____

4. When we reach Galveston, Texas, we needed to get employment.

_____

5. My mom says that I could go out tomorrow night, but first, I had to clean my room.

_____

6. We lit sixteen candles on my birthday cake tomorrow.

_____

7. James and Bob spent the day at the batting cage because there were nothing to do at their house.

_____

8. Cats is very playful, and the children will be chased them often.

_____

9. Robin smile whenever she saw her boyfriend in the hall.

_____

10. While we took the short cut through the woods, Jeremy rides his bike on the street.

_____

11. Garrett Jax will have watching three hours of television by tomorrow.

_____

12. Because Carl Fanders will be underweight, he could not enter the wrestling competition.

_____

13. Regis used his pickax, and, as he strikes the ground, he saw a gold-colored rock.

_____

14. In my mind, Blane were the best chess player on the team.

_____

15. Cadice Torrman will have arriving at the airport by noon on Saturday.

_____

16. We been here for two hours.

_____

17. If you yearned for suspense and adventure, read *Call of the Wild* by Jack London.

_____

18. When Jabari runs the 200 meter race, he set a school record, and he won the race too.

_____

19. Herschel was the student who loses her mother in a car accident.

_____

20. Live a good life in the future, and you were happy.

_____

21. He use a food guide pyramid to eat the right kind of foods.

_____

22. Ms. Logan stated that she was not dismissing classes until each of the students were quiet.

_____

23. Do you like rock 'n' roll, or will you prefer reggae?

_____

24. There were a big bag of peanuts on the shelf.

_____

25. Before we left for vacation, she stay on the telephone for two hours.

_____

For questions 26 – 30, rewrite the sentences so they no longer contain dangling or misplaced modifiers.

26. My mother gave chocolate chip cookies to my friends with pecans in them.

_____

27. By passing the test quickly, your application can be processed this month.

_____

28. Chip threw the baseball to Troy moving slowly.

_____

29. Carrying one basketball under each arm, the coach drilled Kyle.

_____

30. To cause such large weather disturbances, El Niño must be involved.

_____

CHAPTER 4 TEST

Read the sentences below. Choose the correct sentence classification from the list.

1. The avocado hit the tree with such force that the avocado exploded.
   A. simple
   B. compound
   C. complex
   D. compound-complex

2. Wes and Jackie went to the rodeo, but they were surprised by what they saw.
   A. simple
   B. compound
   C. complex
   D. compound-complex

3. Jeff brought his metal bat out of the dugout to try for a home run, but when the lightning started flashing, he had to exchange it for a wooden bat.
   A. simple
   B. compound
   C. complex
   D. compound-complex

4. Lord Byron wrote many important literary works, and several of them are still read today.
   A. simple
   B. compound
   C. complex
   D. compound-complex

5. Larry Barr decided to take us all out to dinner, but I really did not feel like eating.
   A. simple
   B. compound
   C. complex
   D. compound-complex

6. With three minutes to spare, Lester delivered the pizza to the correct house; the pizza was still hot and fresh when he rang the doorbell.
   A. simple   C. complex
   B. compound   D. compound-complex

7. To the right of the door, Stacy and Lennie were holding hands and winking.
   A. simple   C. complex
   B. compound   D. compound-complex

8. Regardless of who will finish first, the point of the game is to have fun.
   A. simple   C. complex
   B. compound   D. compound-complex

9. We will be twisting the rope together while you are feeding the twine to us.
   A. simple   C. complex
   B. compound   D. compound-complex

10. In time with the music, the cricket danced and chirped.
    A. simple   C. complex
    B. compound   D. compound-complex

Read the sentences below. Then decide whether the underlined part is a phrase, an independent clause, or a dependent clause.

11. Take your time <u>when you race around that curve in the road</u>.
    A. phrase   B. independent clause   C. dependent clause

12. Their favorite breakfast is oatmeal and orange juice <u>without the pulp</u>.
    A. phrase   B. independent clause   C. dependent clause

13. While Fernando was gone, <u>his brother left for California</u>.
    A. phrase   B. independent clause   C. dependent clause

14. Laughter lightens life's sorrows and also <u>lifts our spirits</u>.
    A. phrase   B. independent clause   C. dependent clause

15. I will keep myself busy <u>until you return from your trip</u>.
    A. phrase   B. independent clause   C. dependent clause

Each sentence below contains a misplaced modifier. Select the sentence that is rewritten correctly.

16. The tourists were safe from the piranhas in the raft.
    A. The tourists in the piranhas were safe from the raft.
    B. The tourists in the raft were safe from the piranhas.
    C. From the piranhas, the tourists were safe in the raft.
    D. The piranhas were safe from the tourists in the raft.

17. The cat attacked the slimy rat pouncing quickly.
    A. The slimy rat, pouncing quickly, attacked the cat.
    B. The cat attacked, pouncing quickly the slimy rat.
    C. The slimy cat attacked the rat, pouncing quickly.
    D. Pouncing quickly, the cat attacked the slimy rat.

18. Kyle threw the ball to Felicia spinning in the air.
    A. Kyle threw the ball, spinning in the air, to Felicia.
    B. Kyle, spinning in the air, threw the ball to Felicia.
    C. Kyle threw the ball to spinning Felicia.
    D. Felicia was thrown, spinning in the air, to the ball.

19. He works two places so he can pay his bills at night.
    A. So he can pay his bills at night, he works two places.
    B. He works two places at night, so he can pay his bills.
    C. Paying his bills at night, he works two places.
    D. In two places, he works so he can pay his bills.

20. Brad and his friend, Bethany, served the seven course dinner looking well-dressed to the guests.
    A. Looking well-dressed to the guests, the seven course dinner served Brad and his friend, Bethany.
    B. Brad and his friend, Bethany, served the seven course dinner to the guests looking well-dressed.
    C. Brad and his friend, Bethany, served the well-dressed seven course dinner to the guests.
    D. Looking well-dressed, Brad and his friend, Bethany, served the seven course dinner to the guests.

Each sentence below contains a dangling modifier. Select the sentence that is rewritten correctly.

21. After a few years of playing music, medicine became his chosen course of study.
    A. Medicine became his chosen course of study after a few years of playing music.
    B. While playing music, medicine became his chosen course of study.
    C. After he played music for a few years, medicine became his chosen course of study.
    D. He played music a few years after medicine became his chosen course of study.

22. Sailing the raft up the Amazon River, the light guided the explorers to their destination.
    A. Using the light to guide them, the raft was sailed up the Amazon River to their destination.
    B. The explorers, using the light as a guide, sailed the raft up the Amazon River to their destination.
    C. The explorers were using the raft to light their way up the Amazon River to their destination.
    D. The Amazon River was sailed to their destination by the raft using the light to guide them.

23. Wearing a yellow rain jacket, the water found a way inside Vince's clothes.

    A.   Vince was wearing a yellow rain jacket, but the water found a way inside his clothes.

    B.   Vince, wearing a yellow rain jacket, the water found a way inside his clothes.

    C.   The water found a way inside Vince's clothes, which was wearing a yellow rain jacket.

    D.   Wearing a yellow rain jacket, Vince's clothes were found with water inside.

24. Driving to the bank, the family cat meowed at the approaching cars.

    A.   Our family cat, driving to the bank, meowed at approaching cars.

    B.   As we were driving to the bank, our family cat meowed at the approaching cars.

    C.   While meowing at the approaching cars, our family cat was driving to the bank.

    D.   As our family cat meowed at the approaching bank, we were driving to the cars.

25. Unable to endure the damp, cold weather, the sunny South seemed like a good place to live.

    A.   The damp, cold weather in the sunny South seemed like a good place to live.

    B.   Living in the sunny South seemed like a good place to endure the damp, cold weather.

    C.   Although we were unable to endure the sunny South, staying in the damp, cold weather seemed like a good place to live.

    D.   Because we were unable to endure the damp, cold weather, the sunny South seemed like a good place to live.

Chapter 5
Adjectives, Adverbs, Using Negative Words

This chapter references conventions	
ELA 8C1b	analyzes and uses simple, compound, complex, and compound-complex sentences correctly, punctuates properly, and avoids fragments and run-ons
ELA8C1f	analyzes the structure of a sentence (basic sentence parts, noun-adjective-adverb clauses and phrases)

ADJECTIVES

Example: The beautiful aquarium contains a rare kind of seaweed.

In this example, the word **beautiful** refers to the aquarium and answers the question, "*What kind* of aquarium is it?" Also, the word **rare** in this sentence describes the seaweed and answers the question, "*What kind* of seaweed is this?" So, the adjectives in this sentence are **beautiful** and **rare**.

NOTE: Adjectives can also be formed by adding the suffixes *-able, -ful, -ish, -less,* or *-y* to nouns and verbs.

Example: The selfish customer took the Beanie Baby out of the shopping **cart of a helpless child**.

In this example, the word **selfish**, formed by adding *-ish* to *self*, describes what kind of customer is in the store. The word **helpless**, formed by adding the suffix *-less* to *help*, describes the child in the cart.

NOTE: Possessive pronouns such as *his*, *her*, *its*, *our,* and *their* can be used as adjectives. The articles *a*, *an*, and *the* are adjectives. In addition, *this*, *that*, *these*, and *those* can be adjectives.

Practice 1: Adjectives

Read the following sentences, and underline all adjectives.

   Example: Barry Goldstein drove <u>his</u> <u>red</u> pickup truck down <u>the</u> <u>steep</u> side of <u>a</u> mountain.

1. Jerry took his yellow ATV and ran it through the muddiest part of the woods.

2. Tim's girlfriend, Tamara, stared at all the cute, furry animals in the pet store.

3. "If I had a dollar bill for every time I heard that remark, I'd be a millionaire!" Richie said.

4. I left the costume party with wet clothes after slipping on the shiny floor and falling over the red punch bowl.

5. "Just wait till Grandma hears how you broke her new vase!" Jake said to his big brother, Ed.

6. The large piranha ate the scrawny fish.

7. Jacinda joyously played in the yellow daffodils and warmed her beaming face in the sun.

8. The bashful host just looked at the ground when his thoughtful guests applauded him.

9. The embarrassed bride clumsily picked up her fallen veil and continued marching down the aisle.

10. Garrett, the class clown, stuck sharpened pencils into his ears and did other foolish things.

ADVERBS

An **adverb** is the part of speech used to modify (describe) many different kinds of words. Adverbs can modify verbs, adjectives, or other adverbs. Frequently, adverbs end in **-ly**. For example, **lovely, truly,** and **softly** are adverbs. However, be aware of adverbs that do not end   in **-ly** such as **soon, well,** etc.

Adverbs modifying verbs – If an adverb describes a verb, it will answer one of these four questions: **Where? When? In what manner? To what extent?**

   Example 1: Does the musician really understand what he is getting into?
   In this example, the adverb, **really**, answers the question, "*To what extent* does the musician understand?"

   Example 2: Is the storm going to hit our area tomorrow?
   In this example, the adverb, **tomorrow**, answers the question, "*When* could the storm hit?"

Adverbs modifying adjectives – If an adverb describes an adjective, it answers the question, "*To what extent?*"

   Example: With her husband's death, she is now a very wealthy widow.
   In this example, the adverb, **very**, answers the question "*To what extent* is the widow wealthy?"

Adverbs modifying other adverbs – If an adverb describes another adverb, the adverbs will appear together, and the first adverb will answer the question *"To what extent?"* for the second adverb.

> **Example:** The stunt men ride their high-powered motorcycles more cautiously than before. In this example, the adverb, **more**, answers the question, *"To what extent* do the stunt men ride their motorcycles **cautiously**?"

Practice 2: Adverbs

Read the following sentences. Circle all of the adverbs in each sentence. If a sentence does not contain any adverbs, write N in the right margin.

> **Example:** Rod (carefully) picked up the diamond and examined it for flaws.

1. Stephen King's description of the clown in his novel, *It,* is frightening.

2. What should we do today, Amelia?

3. Terry prepared the apple turnovers quickly.

4. After the soldier jammed his gun, he had to clean it extremely well.

5. Our translator can speak both Japanese and English quite fluently.

6. We ate the cookies ravenously while they were still warm.

7. Kerri Fisher's pet rabbit, Fluffy, was finishing a cut carrot.

8. Priscilla was barely able to stand up after getting off the roller coaster.

9. The hyena was cackling loudly to the left of the lion.

10. George Lucas is using his newly-invented digitized sound system called THX in his movies.

COMPARATIVE AND SUPERLATIVE ADJECTIVES AND ADVERBS

Definition 1: The **comparative** form of adjectives and adverbs is used to compare two things.

> **Example 1:** Betty is **taller** than you.
> **Example 2:** Birmingham is **more distant** from us than Gadsden.

NOTE: You must use **than** after a comparative adjective or adverb.

Definition 2: The **superlative** form of adjectives and adverbs is used to compare three or more things.

> **Example 1:** Kurt is the **strongest** wrestler on the team.
> **Example 2:** Atlanta is the **most beautiful** city in Georgia.

Rule 1. **Most of the time, if the adjective or adverb is a one syllable word, *er* and *est* are placed at the end of the word for comparative and superlative forms.**

Example 1: Jake was **smarter** at playing golf than John.

Example 2: Marsha had the **straightest** hair in the family.

Rule 2. In most cases, if adjectives and adverbs have two syllables or more, place *more, most, less,* or *least* in front of the modifier for the comparative and superlative forms.

Example 1: Tito wore the **most expensive** suit at the party.

Example 2: Carrie was **less reliable** than her roommate.

NOTE: Don't use **more** and **-er** with the same adjective.

Example: Saying "Dana is **more brighter** than Doreen" is incorrect.

Rule 3. Adverbs with *-ly* endings and adjectives with more than two syllables are *always* made comparative and superlative by using *more, most, less,* or *least.*

Example 1: The truck was **less heavily** weighted in the front than in the back.

Example 2: Darlene is the **most beautiful** woman in Savannah.

Practice 3: Comparative and Superlative Adjectives and Adverbs

Using rules 1 – 3, underline the correct word(s) in the following sentences.

1. In general, Tom seems to be **quicker / more quick** than Karen.

2. Out of all the witnesses, Randy was **certainest / most certain** about what he saw.

3. The crowd cheered the movie star **wilder / more wildly** than the other two guests.

4. The soup was **deliciousless / less delicious** when shrimp were added to it.

5. People act the **craziest / most crazy** when the moon is full.

6. The road was **visibler / more visible** when the fog lifted.

7. The music was played **softliest / most softly** while dinner was being served.

8. The mouse was **smaller / more small** than the hamster.

9. In her everyday life, Sarah is **bashfullest / most bashful** when she is at school.

10. He was **afraidest / most afraid** of danger when he was alone.

Rule 4. If the comparison is negative, use words such as *worse* (comparing two things) and *worst* (comparing three or more things) as the modifier.

Example 1: The passenger had **worse** injuries after the accident than before.

Example 2: Out of all the competitors, Billy was the **worst** racer.

NOTE: If two items are being compared, the **comparative** form is used. If three or more items are being compared, the **superlative** form is used.

Comparative Example: Katie can sing **better** than I can.

Superlative Example: Katie is the **best** singer in the choir.

Practice 4: More Comparative and Superlative Forms

Using Rule Four and the Note, underline the correct comparative or superlative form that should be used in the following sentences.

1. Katrina keeps a **cleaner / cleanest** room than her sister.

2. Out of all his co-workers, Mr. Nishimura talks the **more / most** fluently.

3. Tabitha does **less / least** singing than dancing.

4. Craig does his chores **more / most** cheerfully than his brother.

5. Considering all of his talents, Angelo is **less / least** able to fix cars.

6. Of the two beds, the more expensive one was **firmer / firmest**.

7. That's the **more / most** amazing thing we've ever seen in our lives!

8. This guitarist plays **less / least** skillfully than his brother.

9. Teachers at our high school do their **better / best** instruction when they are happy.

10. The **newer / newest** of the four pairs of shoes was given to the soccer team's star player.

11. Michelle ran **faster / fastest** than Shannon in the 200 meter race.

12. Since he used to be a server, Gabe was the **more / most** generous tipper in the restaurant.

13. My brother can swim **faster / fastest** than your brother.

14. I can see **better / best** when it is light than when it is dark.

15. My aunt always picks out **sweeter / sweetest** watermelons than my uncle.

Here is a list of irregular comparative and superlative adjectives and adverbs:

Irregular Comparative and Superlative Adjectives and Adverbs

Adj / Adv	Comparative	Superlative
ill	worse	worst
bad	worse	worst
good	better	best
well	better	best
many	more	most
much	more	most
some	more	most
little	less	least

Practice 5: Irregular Comparative and Superlative Adjectives and Adverbs

Read the following sentences. Rewrite the sentence, and correct the irregular comparative or superlative form on the lines below.

1. Carly did worser than me on the test.

   _____

2. Greg is the baddest baseball player on the team.

   _____

3. Jessica Helms is more good at typing than at sewing.

   _____

4. Tanya Brown has little time than Sauren to finish the homework.

   _____

5. The patient felt weller after he had the shot.

   _____

6. Considering all the jobs he had in his lifetime, Abraham Lincoln was more well-known as the president of the United States.

   _____

7. Terrence spent the littler amount of money on himself.

   _____

8. Germaine has taken most of the credit than Alice.

   _____

9. Houston McDonald's behavior is the worse in the class.

   _____

10. Brandie is feeling more ill than Helen today.

    _____

11. I have the most money than Shawn does.

    _____

12. That storm was worst than the one last week.

    _____

13. Joe is the bestest player on the hockey team.

_____

14. Reba has little money than Rubie.

_____

15. She has the mostest charm of anyone I know.

_____

USING NEGATIVE WORDS

In English, two negative words cannot be used to express one negative idea. These two words are referred to as a **double negative.** Yet this mistake is one of the most common errors in English. Commonly used words to express negative ideas include **nothing, no one, neither, none, not, nor, nearly, barely, scarcely, but, never, no, hardly, rarely,** and **seldom.**

Example 1: There is **hardly no one** here.
This sentence is incorrect because the same sentence contains two negatives, **hardly** and **no one.** Here is a correct way to rephrase the sentence: There is **hardly anyone** here.

Example 2: I **didn't** see **nothing** suspicious yesterday.
This sentence is incorrect because two negatives, **not** from the contraction **didn't** and the word **nothing,** are used in the same sentence. Here is one way to correctly write this sentence: I **didn't** see **anything** suspicious yesterday.

Example 3: Stacy **nearly never** has the chance to go bowling.
This sentence is incorrect because the two negatives, **nearly** and **never,** are both used to describe how often Stacy gets to bowl. Correctly stated: Stacy **seldom** has the chance to go bowling.

Practice 6: Using Negative Words

Read the following sentences. If the sentence contains more than one negative word, rewrite the sentence correctly. If the sentence has only one negative word, write C on the line under the sentence.

1. I haven't never seen anything like it!

_____

2. You don't have nothing to show for your efforts.

_____

3. When I looked in the pool, I saw no one.

_____

4. She had barely touched the glass when it fell over.

_____

5. We had scarcely no food left in our supplies.

_____

6. There wasn't never nothing to do at their house.

_____

7. My mother hardly never lets me use her car.

_____

8. I don't need no help on my homework this time.

_____

9. Phillip and Peter drove until there was hardly no gas in the tank.

_____

10. We nearly had to cancel the performance when the leading actress got sick.

_____

11. Joey couldn't find no one to talk to at the party.

_____

12. Trudi hadn't scarcely opened her eyes when the bear walked in.

_____

13. Sergeant Stotts didn't have no ammunition for the coming training exercise.

_____

14. The electric supply was down to barely nothing during the brownout.

_____

15. There wasn't even a quart of jelly left in the pantry.

_____

16. There was barely no one I recognized when the funeral began.

_____

17. Strange as it may seem, Judith spent but none of her lottery winnings on her vacation.

_____

18. From where we were sitting, the performers on stage were not scarcely loud enough to be heard.

    _____

19. Hardly any information can't be found using the computer at school.

    _____

20. Tomorrow no one will never again make war against each other.

    _____

CHAPTER 5 REVIEW

Rewrite each sentence. Correct for errors in comparative, superlative, and double negative forms of adjectives and adverbs.

1. Mr. Stokes hasn't barely begun retirement, the goodest part of his life.

   _____

2. The dolphins seldom swim nowhere near the beach.

   _____

3. Hardly no one checked to see if Sam was having a best time at the party.

   _____

4. The inspector found hardly nothing at the crime scene.

   _____

5. Beth was best at shooting hoops than at sewing dresses.

   _____

6. Steve had hardly never been home all year.

   _____

7. Phil Brown has traced hardly none of his ancestry to the West African Coast.

   _____

8. Lori has not scarcely scratched the surface in understanding her thoughts.

   _____

9. Hardly none of the members of the band are really best at playing their instrument.

   _____

10. Ms. Carlton's bunjee jumping class hardly never had the chance to actually jump.

11. Erica had an extensiver CD collection than her friend, Gabe.

12. Cindy was the more graceful dancer on prom night.

13. This had to be the worse day I have had in my entire life.

14. Jeb played his stereo system more loud than anyone else on his block.

15. Stasia Woods seldom never took out the trash on Sunday night.

16. No one could pitch a baseball gooder than Cedrick.

17. The last man in line did not want to wait for no one.

18. More of them were most interested in our personal lives than in our professional lives.

19. Jennifer was the better shot the team had to beat in the archery competition.

20. Many of the crowd cheered most for the visiting team than for the home team.

21. That particular eagle is the fast bird in the state of Colorado.

22. The foot should not never be used to test the lake for piranhas.

23. Hanna was a more good dancer than her dance partner, Devin.

24. Corrina just nearly found a view of the boxing match by climbing the wall.

_____

25. The ear can hear good when it has been carefully cleaned with warm water.

_____

CHAPTER 5 TEST

Read the following sentences. Select the underlined word which is an *adjective*.

1. Jessie <u>noticed</u> the girl's <u>beautiful</u> <u>dancing</u> and <u>quickly</u> asked her to dance.
   - A. noticed
   - B. beautiful
   - C. dancing
   - D. quickly

2. Howard <u>quickly</u> put cloth strips <u>on</u> the canvas and <u>coated</u> it in tar and pieces of <u>colorful</u> glass.
   - A. quickly
   - B. on
   - C. coated
   - D. colorful

3. "For heaven's <u>sake</u>!" Fran <u>shouted</u>. "You look just like that <u>new</u> actor on <u>television</u>."
   - A. sake
   - B. shouted
   - C. new
   - D. television

4. The <u>childless</u> couple decided to <u>adopt</u> a <u>baby</u> from The People's Republic of <u>China</u>.
   - A. childless
   - B. adopt
   - C. baby
   - D. China

5. <u>Instead of</u> staying at <u>home</u>, the <u>autistic</u> boy took a trip to the <u>zoo</u>.
   - A. Instead of
   - B. home
   - C. autistic
   - D. zoo

6. Muhammad <u>Akbar</u> sailed <u>across</u> the Gulf of Mexico <u>in</u> search of <u>yellow-finned</u> sharks.
   - A. Akbar
   - B. across
   - C. in
   - D. yellow-finned

7. The <u>sleepy</u> town of Elijay, <u>Georgia,</u> is well-known for its mountain <u>charm</u> and <u>beauty</u>.
   - A. sleepy
   - B. Georgia
   - C. charm
   - D. beauty

8. Tanya <u>brought</u> the bashful girl to the <u>front</u> stage so they <u>could</u> do a magic trick <u>together</u>.
   - A. brought
   - B. front
   - C. could
   - D. together

9. Stephen <u>began</u> a <u>long</u> search to <u>find</u> his cousin's <u>ex-roommate</u>, Chris.
   - A. began
   - B. long
   - C. find
   - D. ex-roommate

10. The <u>king</u> <u>smiled</u> a <u>sheepish</u> grin before he rode off on the Arabian <u>horse</u>.
    - A. king
    - B. smiled
    - C. sheepish
    - D. horse

Read the following sentences. Select the underlined word which is an *adverb*.

11. <u>Marcia</u> and Jude <u>danced</u> <u>well</u> together at their <u>friend's</u> party.
    - A. Marcia
    - B. danced
    - C. well
    - D. friend's

12. The <u>highly</u> popular <u>student</u> surprised his friends <u>by</u> talking with the <u>unpopular</u> students.
    - A. highly
    - B. student
    - C. by
    - D. unpopular

13. Given the <u>opportunity</u>, Stacy <u>Billings</u> will return the <u>lost</u> item to its owner <u>soon</u>.
    A. opportunity   B. Billings   C. lost   D. soon

14. <u>By</u> the time the <u>first</u> show <u>finally</u> ended, you were <u>falling</u> asleep in the seat.
    A. By   B. first   C. finally   D. falling

15. "You are <u>naturally</u> quite <u>happy</u> about your <u>coming</u> marriage to <u>your</u> true love," Christy said.
    A. naturally   B. happy   C. coming   D. your

16. The <u>new</u> grading scale <u>will</u> be enforced <u>immediately</u>.
    A. new   B. grading   C. will   D. immediately

17. "<u>Anyone</u> who tries to <u>run</u> this course <u>quickly</u> will get <u>hurt</u>," the drill sergeant said.
    A. Anyone   B. run   C. quickly   D. hurt

18. The <u>very</u> bad <u>actress</u> played a small <u>role</u> in the school's <u>play</u>.
    A. very   B. actress   C. role   D. play

19. "The hamster <u>never</u> gets <u>tired</u> from <u>running</u> inside <u>his</u> play wheel," Shannon said.
    A. never   B. tired   C. running   D. his

20. The <u>differences</u> among <u>ethnic</u> groups are <u>growing</u> <u>more</u> rapidly in the nation today.
    A. differences   B. ethnic   C. growing   D. more

Choose the correct word or phrase to complete the sentence.

21. The strike is _____ than any other I've seen.
    A. most violent   C. violenter
    B. least violent   D. more violent

22. His heart beats _____ than mine.
    A. most rapidly   C. rapider
    B. more rapidly   D. least rapid

23. She _____ speaks in class.
    A. hardly never   C. ever nearly
    B. hardly ever   D. not hardly

24. Bone is _____ than cartilage in the human body.
    A. rigider   C. least rigid
    B. most rigid   D. more rigid

25. The train _____ stops in our city.
    A. nearly never   C. seldom
    B. won't never   D. not ever

Chapter 6
Sentence Errors and Sequencing

This chapter references conventions	
ELA 8C1b	analyzes and uses simple, compound, complex, and compound-complex sentences correctly, punctuates properly, and avoids fragments and run-ons

SENTENCES, SENTENCE FRAGMENTS, AND RUN-ONS

A **sentence** consists of a **subject** and a **verb**. A sentence may contain more than one subject and one verb, but only one subject and one verb are needed to make a sentence.

Examples: The <u>cow</u> (jumped) over the gate.   <u>Willie </u>(was amazed).

Subject Verb   Subject   Verb

A **sentence fragment** is a collection of words that do not express a complete thought.

Example: Waiting for her sister to get the pizza. The best fried chicken in town.

How to fix sentence fragments: To correct a sentence fragment, simply add the parts of the sentence that are missing. If the sentence is missing a subject, add a subject. If the sentence is missing a verb or predicate, add a verb or predicate.

Example 1: All this year's best peaches.

Corrected: All this year's best peaches are headed to the grocery stores.

Example 2: took the long way back to the house.

<u>*Corrected:*</u>   Calvin took the long way back to the house.

A **run-on sentence** occurs when a comma is used in place of a period, semicolon, or comma + coordinating conjunction (**and**, **but**, **or**, **for**, **nor**, **yet**, **so**) to join two complete sentences. Sometimes, all punctuation is omitted between the complete sentences.

Example 1: Lomax took the children to the park Lenetha entertained a friend at home.

Example 2: I wasn't doing my homework, I hadn't been passing my tests in school.

How to fix run-ons: There are three ways to fix run-ons. The first way is to simply add a period to separate the two complete sentences and add a capital letter to the second sentence.

> **Example:** Joseph went to school the dog stayed at home.
>
> *Corrected:* Joseph went to school. The dog stayed at home.

The second way to fix run-ons is to add a semicolon to separate the two complete sentences.

> *Corrected:* Joseph went to school; the dog stayed at home.

The third way to fix run-ons is to add a comma + coordinating conjunction to separate the two complete sentences.

> *Corrected:* Joseph went to school, and the dog stayed at home.

Practice 1: Sentences, Sentence Fragments, and Run-ons

Read the following examples. Tell whether each example is a sentence, run-on, or sentence fragment. If the example is a run-on or a sentence fragment, rewrite it to make it into a proper sentence. Answers will vary. If it is correct, write a C under the sentence.

1. The cat fell out of the tree onto the roof.

   _____

2. Just in time for that midnight snack.

   _____

3. Running all the way up the stairs.

   _____

4. We're going through the house, you should stay outside.

   _____

5. Fishing in the lake brought back childhood memories.

   _____

6. Tracy took the shortcut home she didn't want to walk far in the heat.

   _____

7. At that time, all people will rise up and demand justice.

   _____

8. He was batting left-handed, the ball went deep into right field.

   _____

9. The soccer game begins at noon the players are here an hour early.

   _____

10. Living in this climate under these conditions.

   _____

11. The jungle was unusually quiet.

   _____

12. People moved quickly there was no time to stop.

   _____

13. With one inning left and bases loaded.

   _____

14. They hiked the mountain they saw a squirrel.

   _____

15. The schools closed because of the blizzard, so we played Nintendo™.

   _____

16. We travel in circles there is no end in sight.

   _____

17. Because the car was full of groceries, many of them perishables like ice-cream.

   _____

18. Light was shining through the stained glass window.

   _____

19. By making the trip seem longer than it actually was.

   _____

20. Traveling upstream, they saw several beavers making a dam.

   _____

21. Working hard to improve my grades.

   _____

22. Anna lives in these apartments, so she can walk to school.

   _____

23. To be a loyal friend to her is very important.

   _____

24. A little warmer today.

_____

25. When we see Robin, she will be carrying the new puppy.

_____

ARRANGING IDEAS IN CHRONOLOGICAL ORDER

Chronological order is one way to show that events or ideas are related.

In chronological order, the earliest event or events in time order appear first. Events happening later in time follow after the earlier event or events. In this way, events are arranged in a sequence.

> **Example:** 1. Ray watered the tree.
>
> 2. Ray walked outside.
>
> 3. Ray filled the can with water from the well.

In this example, the time order is 2-3-1. First, Ray walked outside. Then, Ray filled the can with water. Last, Ray watered the tree.

Practice 2: Arranging Ideas in Chronological Order

Read the following groups of sentences. For each group of sentences, decide the correct order of events or ideas. Then use the numbers to write the correct order on the line provided.

A. 1. She slowly watered the soil until the seedlings were soaked.

2. Jasmine made holes two inches apart and planted rosemary seedlings.

3. Jasmine pulled large rocks out of a plot of land.

4. Carefully, she put down a three inch layer of topsoil.

_____

B. 1. Sammy bought a game system for his room.

2. His television was blurry, and he could not see the game as he played.

3. Sammy bought a better television.

4. He followed the directions carefully when he connected the system to his television.

_____

C. 1. One of the windows was broken, and glass was on the seat.

2. We walked to our parked car on the basement level of the hotel.

3. We reported the theft to the police immediately.

4. The car phone and CD player were missing.

_____

D. 1. We cleaned the fish and cooked them on an open fire.

2. We bought some worms and baited our hooks.

3. Gary caught a catfish, and I caught two bass.

4. Gary and I took the day off and decided to go fishing.

SEQUENCING DIRECTIONS IN THE CORRECT ORDER

Directions can also be arranged in a sequence. Each step in the directions follows *chronological order.* When directions are arranged chronologically, the earliest step or steps in time order appear first. Steps happening later in time follow the earlier step or steps.

Example: 1. Come back in two days and pick up the clothes.

2. Take the bag to the dry cleaner.

3. Place all clothes in a laundry bag.

CLEANERS

According to these directions, the time order is 3-2-1. First, you put the clothes in a bag. Then, you take the bag to a dry cleaner. Last, you return in two days to pick up your clothes.

Practice 3: Sequencing Directions in Correct Order

Read the following sentences. For each group of sentences, decide the correct order to make a coherent paragraph. Then write that order on the line provided.

A. 1. Go to the store and buy the ingredients called for in the recipe.

2. Mix all of the ingredients in a mixing bowl.

3. Carefully measure all the ingredients.

4. Roll the cookie dough into 1" balls, and place on a cookie sheet.

_____

B. 1. After stepping inside the car, close the door.

2. Put your foot on the brake and shift the car into reverse.

3. Look out the back window as you leave the garage.

4. Put the key in the ignition, and turn it clockwise.

_____

C. 1. Write a check or money order for the amount you want to purchase.

2. Place the order and the check in an envelope, and mail the envelope.

3. Write the item numbers on the order form, and calculate the cost.

4. Look through the catalog, and write the items you want to buy on a sheet of paper.

_____

D. 1. Find out the location of the personnel office when you reach the company.

2. Make a personal appearance at the company in which you are interested.

3. Ask the person at the personnel office for an application.

4. Return the completed application to the personnel office.

_____

CHAPTER 6 REVIEW

Correct the following sentence fragments and run-ons. Answers will vary. Write C if there is no error.

1. Until the captain gives the order.

_____

2. She was staring out the window she didn't notice what the teacher was saying.

_____

3. By looking in the kitchen, Carrie noticed that Ken, Chris, and Robert were playing cards while Ken's little brother was drinking root beer.

_____

_____

4. Stephen plays the tuba in marching band, he has to maintain a 2.5 GPA in order to stay in the marching band.

_____

_____

5. By the time your friend turns on her computer and gets my e-mail.

_____

6. Daniel is stepping on Keri's toes, Keri wants Daniel to stop dancing; Bobby is dancing perfectly with his girlfriend, Kathy.

_____

_____

7. Travis Tritt is performing a concert on the 25th, I hope my friend, Charlie, can go, but he usually goes out of town on the weekends.

_____

_____

8. A large termite-infested log in the middle of the gravel road.

_____

9. Her magazine article declaring an end to racism in the workplace was very well-written this article effectively reached a large audience of influential people in the United States.

_____

_____

10. The sky was turning a dark purple the wind was blowing very softly.

_____

11. Right side of the door.

_____

12. Roller blade races at the park.

_____

13. Sheri saw the light it shined very brightly.

_____

14. He drove with no destination in mind.

_____

15. The horses galloped the riders spurred them on.

_____

Reorder the sentence groups below (numbers 16 – 25) into correct sequential order.

16. 1. After he got his receipt, Frank left the store with the football.

 2. Frank asked the clerk where he could find the footballs.

 3. Frank walked into Mike's Sporting Goods looking for a football.

 4. He selected a football and then went to the cashier to pay for it.

 _____

17. 1. Tape the wrapping paper together so that the paper will stay on the gift.

 2. Tape a card or a bow to the top of the wrapped gift.

 3. Buy wrapping paper, scissors, sec-through tape, and a card or bow at the local drugstore.

 4. Cover the gift with wrapping paper, and cut off the excess paper.

 _____

18. 1. Attach your favorite bait to the hook.

 2. Wait for the bobber to disappear under the water before reeling in the fish.

 3. Cast the line into the lake, stream, or river.

 4. Attach three sinkers, one hook, and one bobber to the fishing line.

 _____

19. 1. He took one step and jumped off the tower.

 2. Jack climbed up the tower.

 3. He fastened the bungee cord to his legs before he jumped.

 4. Jack got instructions on how to jump when he was on the ground.

 _____

20. 1. Third on the list of popularity in the poll was a businesswoman, Patricia Giles.

 2. The candidate most likely to win was the incumbent, Jack Stern.

 3. The candidate least likely to win was Sam Hutchinson, the Libertarian candidate.

 4. Right behind the incumbent was the democratic candidate, Bill Seward.

 _____

21. 1. Do not leave the waiting room until your name is called.

2. Make an appointment over the phone to see a doctor.

3. Pay for services rendered.

4. Sign in at the reception desk at the time of your appointment.

_____

22. 1. The guests paid their check and left a tip.

2. The hostess found a table for the party of four.

3. The server brought out the ordered meal and the check.

4. The server wrote down the guests' order.

_____

23. 1. When the drying cycle is finished, take out your clothes and fold them immediately.

2. Turn on the washing machine for the appropriate water level and temperature setting.

3. Place all clothes of similar color together into the washing machine.

4. Take the clothes out of the washer and place them in the dryer.

_____

24. 1. The boy picked up his toothbrush.

2. The boy gargled water and spit into the sink.

3. The boy brushed his teeth, gums, and tongue.

4. Very carefully, he spread the toothpaste onto the toothbrush.

_____

25. 1. Gather a large supply of dead branches in the forest.

2. Use a flint or match to light the kindling.

3. Add smaller twigs first, and then add larger branches.

4. Use pine straw and dead leaves as kindling.

_____

CHAPTER 6 TEST

Read the directions for each section of the test, and carefully read the four choices for each question.

For questions 1 – 4, select the grammatically correct *complete sentence* in each word group by circling A, B, C, or D.

1.
- A. By the time he left.
- B. At odds with her surroundings.
- C. In the center of the aisle.
- D. The worker poured the concrete.

2.
- A. In the middle of the night.
- B. Daisies were swaying in the breeze
- C. No one's fault.
- D. By remaining silent.

3.
- A. Racing past each other.
- B. The competition was fierce.
- C. Bypassing the other road.
- D. With the transmission in second gear.

4.
- A. Although the lights were out.
- B. Just in time to see the wedding take place.
- C. With no time to spare.
- D. The rain made traveling difficult.

For questions 5 – 8, select the *sentence fragment* in each word group by circling A, B, C, or D.

5.
- A. She flew to an island resort.
- B. Repeating the same long story.
- C. The horses were enjoying the day.
- D. Some people didn't leave.

6.
- A. With her hands on her hips.
- B. I dropped the quarter into the machine.
- C. Jake ran to the fire station and begged for their assistance.
- D. Many people were concerned about the food shortage in their area.

7.
- A. The skaters performed many graceful moves.
- B. Before I could say goodbye, she was gone.
- C. The biggest bully in town.
- D. I bought the car we looked at.

8.
- A. We took turns dancing the Irish jig.
- B. Many people decided to go.
- C. Staring into the dirty window.
- D. The singing got better and better.

For questions 9 –11, select the grammatically correct *complete sentence* in each word group by circling A, B, C, or D.

9. A.   The jungle was unusually quiet as we traveled through it.
   B.   I went to the grocery store today, I stopped at the pet shop.
   C.   The rain stopped for awhile then started up again.
   D.   Mountains of pine trees and beautiful meadows.

10. A.   The couples were dancing as the country music played.
    B.   Six of us went to Dallas, we encountered a terrible flood on our way there.
    C.   The fishing was good the bait was not.
    D.   The ride continued it was quick and jerky.

11. A.   The weather was rough we played chess.
    B.   The shuttle was slow it had no fuel.
    C.   Although he changed the spark plugs, the vehicle refused to run.
    D.   The pews were polished for the wedding they looked very shiny.

For questions 12 –15, select the *run-on sentence* in each group by circling A, B, C, or D.

12. A.   Give me the keys, and I'll start the car.
    B.   If I remove the wall, can you clean up the mess?
    C.   William flew the kite well the wind was calm.
    D.   After the dishes are done, we will watch the movie.

13. A.   Before I dressed for work, I called my best friend.
    B.   Both Dan and Don attend Boy Scout meetings.
    C.   For her part in the play, she received an award for best leading actress.
    D.   Terry flew to San Francisco, his camera was still in Mexico City.

14. A.   The sky was full of clouds; it was going to rain.
    B.   Jamie went to the movies, he bought popcorn.
    C.   The weather was beautiful, so we decided to walk.
    D.   After we ate, we had dessert.

15. A.   After the circus performance, we took the kids out for ice cream.
    B.   My mother took the prescription drug the headache left her immediately.
    C.   The dance floor was packed with people, so we decided to go outside.
    D.   The thief took the jewelry, but he left his fingerprints on the jewelry case.

For questions 16 – 20, select the arrangement of sentences that give *sequential order*.

16. 1. Jerry hit the ball with all his might.

　2. Jerry stepped up to the plate with bases loaded.

　3. The pitcher threw a curve ball to Jerry's right.

　4. Jerry's team gained four runs with his home run.

　A.　4, 2, 3, 1　　　　B.　2, 1, 3, 4　　　　C.　3, 4, 2, 1　　　　D.　2, 3, 1, 4

17. 1. Derek stole the basketball out of Sam's hands.

　2. Eric threw the basketball into the basket.

　3. Sam dribbled the basketball to the other side of the court.

　4. Derek passed the basketball to Eric.

　A.　3, 4, 2, 1　　　　B.　2, 3, 1, 4　　　　C.　3, 1, 4, 2　　　　D.　1, 3, 2, 4

18. 1. Melba heated the vegetable oil in the frying pan.

　2. Melba mixed together eggs, milk, flour, and baking soda.

　3. Melba placed an eight inch stack of pancakes on the table.

　4. She spooned the batter into the pan and fried the pancakes.

　A.　4, 1, 3, 2　　　　B.　1, 2, 3, 4　　　　C.　3, 2, 4, 1　　　　D.　1, 2, 4, 3

19. 1. A mudslide started to the left of the hikers.

　2. The hikers were climbing up the mountain in bright sunshine.

　3. The hikers ran down the mountain for safety.

　4. A rainstorm passed over the mountain.

　A.　2, 1, 3, 4　　　　B.　2, 4, 1, 3　　　　C.　3, 4, 2, 1　　　　D.　1, 4, 2, 3

20. 1. Go to the pound and look at the animals.

　2. Choose a pet that you think will be right for your family.

　3. Take your new pet home and love it.

　4. Take your choice to the "get acquainted" area and make sure you are compatible.

　A.　4, 2, 3, 1　　　　B.　1, 2, 4, 3　　　　C.　3, 2, 4, 1　　　　D.　1, 4, 2, 3

For questions 21 – 25, select the arrangement that gives the directions in *logical order*.

21. 1. Check in your luggage at the airline customer counter.

　2. Purchase your plane tickets in advance over the phone using a credit card.

　3. Find your boarding gate and board the plane.

　4. Arrive at the airport one hour early.

　A.　2, 1, 3, 4　　　　B.　2, 4, 1, 3　　　　C.　3, 4, 2, 1　　　　D.　1, 2, 3, 4

22. 1. Drive to the window and pay for your meal.

2. Pull into a drive-through restaurant.

3. Read the display menu and order your meal.

4. Make sure you receive everything you ordered.

A.   3, 4, 2 1   B.   2, 3, 1, 4   C.   2, 3, 4, 1   D.   3, 1, 4, 2

23. 1. Read all choices before answering a multiple-choice question.

2. If you can't decide on an answer, skip it and move on.

3. When you finish the test, return to the skipped questions.

4. Cross out choices that you know are incorrect.

A.   4, 2, 3, 1   B.   1, 4, 3, 2   C.   3, 2, 4, 1   D.   1, 4, 2, 3

24. 1. Turn on the computer and the monitor.

2. When finished, remove the disk and turn off the computer.

3. Make sure the monitor and the computer are plugged in.

4. When prompted by the computer, place the program disk into the A drive.

A.   3, 4, 2, 1   B.   2, 3, 1, 4   C.   3, 1, 4, 2   D.   1, 3, 2, 4

25. 1. Pour the mix into the pan.

2. Mix together the brownie mix, milk, and oil until well-blended.

3. Place the pan into the oven for 22 minutes.

4. Grease the 9×13 pan, and preheat the oven.

A.   4, 1, 3, 2   B.   1, 2, 3, 4   C.   4, 2, 1 3   D.   2, 1, 4, 3

Chapter 7
Spelling

This chapter references conventions	
ELA8C1g	produces final drafts/presentations that demonstrate accurate spelling and the correct use of punctuation and capitalization

SPELLING AFFIXED WORDS

Affixed words are words that have had a suffix or prefix added to them.

- A **prefix** is a group of letters that are placed **before** a root word.
- A **root** is a basic part of a word that can have a prefix or suffix added to it.
- A **suffix** is a group of letters that are placed **after** a root word.

Here are some examples of common prefixes and suffixes and their meanings:

Prefix	Meaning	Example	Suffix	Meaning	Example
de-	take away from	derail demerit	-dom	place or state of being	kingdom freedom
bi-	two	bipolar	-ism	doctrine belief	atheism
inter-	between	international	-acy	state or quality	accuracy
un-	not	unstoppable	-ate	cause to be	appreciate
hyper-	over, more than	hyperactive	-able, ible	capable of being	livable
semi-	half	semisweet	-ive	having the nature of	explosive festive
micro-	tiny	microscope	-sion, -tion	state of being or action	locomotion fusion
dis-	apart, away	disorder	-ful	having a quality	bashful
il-, im-, in-, ir-	not	immature irreverent	-ious, ous	of or characterized by	delicious zealous
pre-	before	preheat	-less	without	colorless

NOTE: Because the English language draws from many other language sources, there are many irregularities in spelling when affixes are added to base words. Please consult a reference source for a complete list of spellings of words and their affixes.

Here are some common roots and their meanings:

Root	Meaning	Example	Root	Meaning	Example
mis	to send	admission	uni	one	unite
hydro	water	hydroplane	satis	sufficient	satisfaction
duc	to lead	produce	port	to carry	transport
scrib	to write	subscribe	vis	to see	television
audi	to hear	audio	psych	soul	psychology
geo	earth	geometry	tele	far away	telegraph
manu	hand	manual	phil	love	philosopher
jur, jus	law	jury	photo	light	photography

SPELLING RULES FOR AFFIXED WORDS

Rule 1.   Use i before e, except after c, or when a word is pronounced "ay" as in reign.

> **Example:** neighbor, receive, eight, perceive

Exceptions: Most of the time, rule #1 gives someone the correct spelling of a word. However, there are some words that do not follow this rule: **foreigner, forfeit, height, leisure, neither, science, scientific, seizes,** and **weird.**

Rule 2.   When prefixes are added to root words, the spelling of the root word does not change.

> **Example:** dis + satisfied = dissatisfied   un + noticed = unnoticed

Rule 3.   When a suffix starting with a vowel is added to a word ending in a silent e, such as receive and smile, the e is dropped, making words such as receiving and smiling.

Exception 1: The -e is kept if the suffix begins with a consonant.

> **Example:** love + ly = lovely   brave + ness = braveness

Exception 2: The e is not dropped when it would change the meaning of the root word.

> **Example:** dye + ing = dyeing (not dying)   singe + ing = singeing (not singing)

Exception 3: The e is not dropped if the e clarifies pronunciation.

> **Example:** flee + ing = fleeing (not fleing)   toe + ing = toeing (not toing)

Exception 4: The e is not dropped if the sound c or g must be kept soft.

> **Example:** notice + able = noticeable (not noticable)
>
> courage + ous = courageous (not couragous)

Practice 1: Spelling Affixed Words

Correct the spelling errors in the following sentences. Rewrite the misspelled word in the blank to the right of the sentence. If the words are spelled correctly, write C.

1. Samuel is becomeing more bilingual every day. _____

2. Griffin and Mark did many things that were forgiveable as children. _____

3. The winner of the beauty contest was still unnamed. _____

4. The rumors told about Jessica in school were outragous. _____

5. We wrote in our journals after we planed the birthday party. _____

6. Our lovable friend, Christy, bought the balloons and party favors for us. _____

7. Flossing regularly is an excellent way to prevent cavities. _____

8. Interacial harmony in our community is a top priority. _____

9. Table salt is also considered a preservative. _____

10. Russell showed his courage when he saved that girl from drowning. _____

Rule 4. When a suffix starting with a consonant is added to a word ending in a silent e, the e is usually kept, such as in largely and excitement.

Rule 5. When a suffix is added to root words ending in y, change the y to an i, such as in silliness and beautiful.

Exception 1: Keep the **y** if the suffix being added is **-ing**.

   Example: fly + ing = flying (not fliing)   try + ing = trying (not triing)

Exception 2: Keep the **y** if a vowel in the root word comes before the **y**.

   Example: stay + ed = stayed (not staied)   play + ful = playful (not plaiful)

Exception 3: Keep the **y** in some one syllable base words.

   Example: dry + ness = dryness (not driness)   shy + er = shyer (not shier)

Rule 6. If a word ends in a consonant + vowel + consonant, the suffix begins with a vowel. Also, if the word contains only one syllable or an accented ending syllable, double the final consonant. Otherwise, do not double the last consonant in the root.

   Example: stop + er = stopper   begin + ing = beginning   sun + ed = sunned

Rule 7. English words that have French, Greek, Latin, or Italian roots form the plural according to their language.

   Examples:

Singular	Plural	Singular	Plural
analysis	analyses	fungus	fungi
basis	bases	medium	media
beau	beaux	phenomenon	phenomena

Practice 2: Spelling Errors

Correct the spelling errors in the following sentences. If the sentences have no spelling errors, write C.

1. Many people were barely interested in the lecture.

_____

2. She was inable to stop the presses from printing the story.

_____

3. The town mayer read the announcement of the impending invasion.

_____

4. The family was excited to have their own beautyful home.

_____

5. The council presented plans to the mayor for unifying the city neighborhoods.

_____

6. The first graders were exerciseing at the gym.

_____

7. Nan's joke was terribly funny to us.

_____

8. Lori thought Jake should put his gum in a wraper.

_____

9. Angel's horse was tyed to the pole.

_____

10. The father got a plaiful tug from his three-year-old son.

_____

11. My sister cryd when our dog, Fluffy, died.

_____

12. Lance will be flying home this Wednesday.

_____

13. Claire's freinds are picking out the cutest boys in school today.

_____

14. Melissa chose to paint her nails biege.

_____

15. Louie and his sister, Katrina, are liveing at 365 N. Eight Street.

_____

The following is a list of the 100 most commonly misspelled words in the English language. Review these words carefully, and then review the expanded list of misspelled words starting on the next page.

again	course	him	people	things
all right	cousin	interesting	pretty	thought
always	decided	its	received	threw
an	didn't	it's	running	through
and	different	jumped	said	to
animals	dropped	knew	school	together
another	every	know	some	too
around	February	let's	something	tried
asked	first	license	sometimes	two
babies	for	like	started	until
beautiful	friend	little	stopped	very
because	friends	many	surprise	wanted
before	frightened	money	swimming	went
believe	from	morning	than	were
bought	getting	mother	that's	when
came	going	name	their	where
caught	happening	named	then	with
children	hear	off	there	woman
clothes	heard	once	they	would
coming	here	our	they're	you're

Review this expanded list of commonly misspelled words. Have a partner or friend dictate these words to you. See how many you can spell correctly. Learn the spellings of the ones you misspelled.

abandon	among	became	chair	contest
ability	amount	because	change	contract
about	angle	become	channel	contrast
above	animal	being	chapter	contribute
absence	annoy	believe	charge	convention
abundant	answer	bicycle	chart	cooperate
accent	anybody	birthday	check	corner
accept	anything	board	chick	correct
acceptance	apology	body	children	cost
account	appear	boil	choice	cotton
accurate	appetite	bone	choir	couldn't
acid	apple	bonus	choose	count
acquaint	application	border	chorus	country
acquire	apply	bottom	chose	county
across	appointment	boy	circle	coupon
action	approve	brain	circus	course
actor	aren't	bread	citizen	cousins
actual	argument	breakfast	city	credit
addition	arrange	breath	clay	critical
address	arrival	breathe	clearance	cross
adequate	artery	bright	climate	cube
adjust	article	bring	climb	culture
admission	ask	broke	close	currency
adult	assembly	brother	cloth	current
advance	assign	budget	clothing	customer
advantage	artery	build	clouds	damage
adventure	assist	built	coal	dance
advertise	assure	burst	coin	dangerous
advice	ate	business	collect	dark
advise	athletic	busy	colonel	date
affect	attach	buy	color	day
afford	attachment	cabinet	column	death
afraid	attend	cafeteria	come	debate
after	audience	calendar	command	debt
afternoon	author	calf	commit	decide
again	autumn	can't	committee	decimal
age	average	cancel	communicate	decision
agent	awful	cancer	communism	declare
agreeable	awkward	cannot	company	deduct
agreement	baby	capable	compare	defendant
air	balance	capitol	composition	define
airplane	balloon	care	comprehend	definition
Alabama	ballot	carry	concentrate	delay
almost	bank	cashier	concern	delicious
alone	barn	catch	conflict	delivery
alphabet	baseball	caught	congratulate	democracy
already	basic	caution	congress	deny
although	basket	cent	connection	depart
ambition	bear	century	consider	depend
amendment	beautiful	certain	consumer	deposit

description	education	flood	hadn't	insurance
desert	effect	floor	half	interest
dessert	either	flower	hall	interior
determine	elect	fold	handkerchiefs	introduce
develop	election	follow	happen	invert
diagram	electricity	football	happy	isn't
dictionary	elementary	forbid	hard	it's
didn't	employ	force	hardly	its
died	employee	forecast	hasn't	join
different	employer	foreman	have	journey
difficult	energy	forest	haven't	joy
dinner	English	forever	health	judge
diploma	enjoy	forget	hear	jump
direction	enough	forward	heard	jury
dirt	enroll	found	heart	kept
disaster	entrance	fourth	heat	kind
discount	environment	fraction	heavy	kitchen
discovery	equal	freedom	height	knee
discuss	error	friend	help	knew
disease	essay	frog	herd	knife
dishes	evening	front	here	knit
display	ever	fruit	heroes	knock
distance	every	fuel	high	knot
disturb	everybody	full	history	know
divide	everyone	funny	holiday	knowledge
division	everything	furniture	horrible	known
doctor	example	gallon	hospital	label
does	except	game	hour	labor
doesn't	excuse	garden	house	ladder
doing	executive	gas	human	lake
dollar	expect	general	hundred	lamb
don't	expense	generous	hungry	language
done	experience	gentleman	hurry	large
donkey	explain	geography	hurt	larger
double	express	giant	I'll	later
dozen	eye	give	I'm	laugh
draw	face	given	I've	laundry
dress	fact	glass	identify	law
drink	factory	goes	ignorant	leaf
drive	fair	government	immensely	learn
driver	fall	governor	imperfect	learned
dry	family	graduation	important	least
duck	fast	grammar	impress	leave
due	father	grass	improve	legal
during	favorite	grateful	inches	legislature
each	federal	grief	include	length
ear	feel	groceries	income	less
early	feet	group	indent	lesson
earn	female	grown	independence	letter
earth	fence	guess	information	library
east	field	guest	initial	life
easy	finish	guide	inquire	light
eat	first	gulf	inside	line
economy	fish	habit	instead	liquid

literature	nature	peace	profession	residence
live	need	pencil	profit	resource
living	neither	penny	promise	respect
local	nephew	people	promotion	responsible
locate	nerve	perfect	pronounce	result
look	new	perform	prove	retail
loud	newspaper	period	provide	return
lovely	niece	permanent	publish	revise
lunch	night	permit	punctuation	revive
lung	noise	person	pupil	right
machine	noon	phone	purchase	river
magnet	normal	picnic	purpose	rough
mail	north	picture	pursue	ruler
majority	nothing	piece	quart	rural
male	number	pitcher	quarter	safety
many	numeral	place	question	said
march	nurse	plain	quick	salary
market	observe	plan	quiet	salt
marry	occasion	planet	quite	satisfactory
material	occupation	play	quotation	save
mathematics	occupy	please	rabbit	saving
matter	occur	plenty	race	say
may	ocean	plural	radio	scale
maybe	office	point	rate	scene
measure	often	poison	reach	scenery
mechanic	omit	political	read	schedule
medicine	on	politician	ready	school
member	once	pollute	really	science
memory	opinion	population	reason	scientist
mention	opposite	porch	receipt	sea
middle	order	portion	receive	search
mile	organize	position	recess	season
milk	other	postage	recipe	section
mineral	ounce	potatoes	region	security
minute	outline	poultry	register	seldom
Miss	owe	pound	regular	select
mission	own	pour	regulation	semester
mistake	packed	poverty	relative	senate
money	page	predict	remain	senator
month	paid	prefer	remark	send
moon	paint	prefix	remedies	senior
morning	panel	present	remember	sensible
mother	paper	president	remove	sentence
motor	parent	pretend	repair	separate
mountain	park	prevent	repay	sergeant
mouse	part	price	repeat	serious
Mr.	party	primary	replace	service
Mrs.	pass	principal	represent	session
multiply	past	principle	republic	several
muscle	patient	print	request	sheet
music	patriotic	problem	require	shelf
musical	pause	process	rescue	shouldn't
nation	payment	proclaim	research	sight

signature
silence
similar
since
sincerely
single
singular
site
sitting
situation
sketch
skill
skin
small
smile
smooth
snow
society
soil
sold
solid
solve
someone
sometime
sound
soup
south
southern
space
spare
speak
special
speech
spell
spend
spoke
sport
spring
square
stage
stair
star
start
state
statement
station
steady
steam
step
stomach
storm
story
straight

street
stroke
strong
student
studio
study
subject
submit
subscribe
substitute
subtract
succeed
success
sudden
suggestion
summary
summer
sunny
supervisor
supplies
supply
suppose
surprise
survival
survive
swallow
system
table
task
tax
teach
teacher
teeth
television
temperature
temporary
test
than
thank
their
themselves
there
thermometer
they're
thought
throat
through
ticket
time
title
to
together
tomato

tomorrow
tonight
too
took
tooth
tornado
total
toward
town
toy
trade
traffic
tragic
train
transfer
transportation
travel
treaty
trip
truck
truth
tunnel
turkey
twice
two
typewriter
typical
understand
undertake
unite
United States
universe
until
upon
urban
urgent
use
useful
usually
vacancy
vacant
vacation
valley
valuable
value
variety
various
vegetable
vein
verse
version
very
veto

vicinity
victim
view
visit
visitor
vocabulary
vocation
voice
volcano
volume
vote
wages
wait
watch
water
we're
weather
week
weight
welcome
weren't
west
when
whether
which
while
whole
width
wind
window
winter
withhold
woman
women
won't
wood
word
work
worker
working
would
wouldn't
wrist
write
writing
written
wrong
wrote
yard
year
yesterday
yield
you're

you've
your
youth
zero
zone

Various forms of the spelling list can also be tested, including the addition of prefixes and suffixes

Practice 3: Spelling Errors

Select the word in each list that is not spelled correctly.

1.
   A. health   B. moved   C. Southwest   D. autum
2.
   A. floral   B. thirdy-eight B. worker   D. money
3.
   A. scant   B. connection   C. ajust   D. ignorant
4.
   A. withold   B. repeat   C. grand   D. cancel
5.
   A. mathmatics B. wrist   C. charity   D. transportation
6.
   A. happy   B. least   C. envert   D. shelf
7.
   A. opposite   B. regulashun   C. cooperate   D. life
8.
   A. communicate B. geography   C. delicious   D. elementry
9.
   A. vote   B. vegetable   C. agreement   D. I'll
10.
   A. poultry   B. effect   C. inquire   D. attattchment
11.
   A. interior   B. yellow   C. question   D. recieve
12.
   A. owe   B. satisfactery C. tornado   D. vocabulary
13.
   A. promotion   B. clearance   C. enviroment   D. handkerchiefs
14.
   A. becaus   B. laundry   C. cotton   D. isn't
15.
   A. knowledge   B. profession   C. sleeping   D. typewriter
16.
   A. ocaision   B. odorless   C. irreverent   D. orange

Practice 4: Spelling Errors

Read the following sentences. Select the underlined word in each sentence that is misspelled.

1. The legislature is a very important part of the goverment.
   A. legislature B. very   C. important   D. goverment

2. I want to use the macrowave oven to improve the taste of this horrible food.
   A. macrowave   B. improve   C. taste   D. horrible

3. The industrial air filter business has been booming since the enviroment has become regulated by the government.
   A. business   B. booming   C. enviroment   D. government

4. The <u>insurance</u> <u>company</u> thought the <u>intereor</u> <u>damage</u> was slight.
   A. insurance   B. company   C. intereor   D. damage

5. The <u>convention</u> was a large <u>sucsess</u> because everyone could <u>communicate</u> in <u>English</u>.
   A. convention   B. sucsess   C. communicate   D. English

6. Dr. Thorndike's <u>speech</u> on <u>communism</u> and the <u>economy</u> was very <u>intresting</u>.
   A. speech   B. communism   C. economy   D. intresting

7. That <u>vocano</u> <u>forced</u> many <u>people</u> to leave <u>everything</u> behind.
   A. vocano   B. forced   C. people   D. everything

8. Tom gave his <u>bicycle</u> to <u>Miss</u> Hathaway <u>dering</u> <u>lunch</u>.
   A. bicycle   B. Miss   C. dering   D. lunch

9. I <u>prefer</u> to <u>vakation</u> near the <u>ocean</u> when it is <u>sunny</u>.
   A. prefer   B. vakation   C. ocean   D. sunny

10. "The <u>laundry</u> in the <u>delivry</u> <u>truck</u> is on fire!" the <u>nurse</u> screamed.
    A. laundry   B. delivry   C. truck   D. nurse

IDENTIFYING CORRECTLY SPELLED HOMONYMS

Homonyms are words that sound alike but have different meanings and spellings. There are many homonyms in the English language. However, there are several pairs or trios that frequently are misused by students. Practice writing these homonyms in sentences. Your teacher or other students can then check to see if you are using them correctly.

Common Problem Homonyms

its it's	possessive form if *it* contraction of *it has* or *it is*	to too two	in the direction of as well, besides, also one more than one
right rite write	true; opposite of left a solemn act to form or inscribe on a surface	who's whose	contraction of *who is* or *who has* possessive form of *who*
their there they're	possessive form of *they* in that place contraction of *they are*	your you're	belonging to you contraction of you are
cents sense	1/100 of a dollar verb: to feel or experience noun: a feeling or perception	plain plane	flat stretch of land; east to discern airplane; flat surface
bear bare	noun: a large, heavy mammal verb: to suffer or endure without covering, naked	one won	the first number to have gained; to have had success over others
counsel council	advice, to advise leadership group		

Practice 5: Homonyms

Read the following sentences. Rewrite the sentences if homonyms are used incorrectly. If the word usage is correct, write C on the line.

1. We turned the car to the rite and entered the highway.

   _____

2. Terrell Davis went too the store to by some bagels.

   _____

3. Their were so many colors to choose from, we could not decide.

   _____

4. The bare was eating honey in the park.

   _____

5. Whose coat was left at the party?

   _____

6. Mrs. Crosby one a new car on the game show.

   _____

7. It is said he doesn't have enough cents to come in out of the rain.

   _____

8. The planes were full of corn and wheat fields.

   _____

9. They're car was smashed up, but they weren't hurt.

   _____

10. Does Samantha know that your driving to the party?

    _____

11. I can only go there if a group goes.

    _____

12. The officer said, "You have the write to remain silent."

    _____

13. The dog was found with a collar around it's neck.

    _____

14. Their going to the car show tomorrow.

    _____

Chapter 7 Review

Rewrite the following sentences and correct all misspelled words.

1. You're the only reeson I enroled in that group.

   _____

2. Our helth improved when we moved to the Southwest in Febuary.

   _____

3. Wear did Jimmy Dwire go after the wedding?

   _____

4. Sylvia is becoming imensely popular with her clasmates.

   _____

5. The student went to detention for righting notes in class.

   _____

6. The teacher gave the most responsable student extra credit.

   _____

7. Carlos Ibarra drove to the ofice and asked for employment informasion.

   _____

8. Casey became very welthy after she bought a poltry farm.

   _____

9. Can you tell me weather or not this student dictionary is up-to-date?

   _____

10. The docter was praised for her good cents after the sergery.

    _____

11. Blair Dunaway gave you the position as team captain becaus you are a very bold leader.

    _____

12. If you want another popscicle, ask for a yeller one.

    _____

13. Jerry Spitz lost his liscense when he was caught racing his car.

_____

14. A commercial selling thermomiters was playing on my tellevision.

_____

15. The woman's close looked very intristing.

_____

16. Swimming though the ocean is very dangerous during shark seasen.

_____

17. Dwayne looked very aukward when he spilled his shake on the cafteria bully.

_____

18. Our Inglish teacher impresed us with her knoledge of Colonial literature.

_____

19. The high school alumnuses returned for thier ten year reunion.

_____

20. In 1943, Japan's empyre ecstended from Eastern China too the Aleutian Ilands.

_____

21. Faye's new permnent really makes her hair look frizzy.

_____

22. In most of the United States, typerighters are now a thing of the past.

_____

23. I gave the riegns over to Jeanine so she could ride the stallion.

_____

24. Doug through the shot put a great distanse wenever he practiced.

_____

25. All of the extra grosheries were given to needy famlies.

_____

CHAPTER 7 TEST

Read the directions carefully for each section.

For questions 1–12, select the word in each group that is *not* spelled correctly.

1.
   A. learned   B. yellow   C. afternoon   D. thirdy-sic

2.
   A. occaision   B. height   C. conflict   D. timely

3.
   A. multiply   B. twenty-nine C. fruitiest   D. Febuary

4.
   A. Alabama   B. Mrs.   C. orang   D. I've

5.
   A. wood   B. awkward   C. imperfect   D. withold

6.
   A. improve   B. fungis   C. learned   D. session

7.
   A. memory   B. machine   C. mission   D. faverite

8.
   A. executiv   B. mineral   C. fourteenth   D. reckless

9.
   A. swallow   B. temprary   C. urgent   D. determine

10.
   A. sinceerly   B. eye   C. patriotic   D. composition

11.
   A. syllabi   B. admission   C. aplication   D. fraction

12.
   A. organize   B. knock   C. cooperate   D. rimember

For questions 13 – 25, select the <u>underlined</u> word in each sentence that is misspelled.

13. The <u>visitor</u> had <u>horible</u> <u>breath</u>, and his <u>language</u> was equally awful.

   A. visitor   B. horible   C. breath   D. language

14. The supervisor's plan to achieve a promotion in three weeks is inrealistic.

    A. supervisor's   B. plan   C. promotion   D. inrealistic

15. My adventure came erly when the cafeteria door burst open.

    A. adventure   B. erly   C. cafeteria   D. burst

16. The nurse on the third floor has an English accent to.

    A. nurse   B. English   C. accent   D. to

17. The customer congradulated the mechanic for repairing his damaged car.

    A. customer   B. congradulated   C. mechanic   D. damaged

18. The corupt politician began his lecture by flattering his guests.

    A. corupt   B. politician   C. lecture   D. flattering

19. Mrs. Fielding's daughter included a check in her letter to her freind.

    A. Mrs.   B. daughter   C. included   D. freind

20. For some unknown reason, everyone was dansing in the shopping mall.

    A. unknown   B. everyone   C. dansing   D. shopping

21. Mr. Sargrave's sincere speech made Sylvester smile satisfactrily.

    A. sincere   B. speech   C. smile   D. satisfactrily

22. The payments on the interest were now larger than the payments on the princple.

    A. payments   B. interest   C. larger   D. princple

23. Tonight's special at the steak house is marinated shicken

    A. special   B. house   C. marinated   D. shicken

24. Sylvara was a beutiful acrobat who had perfect balance.

    A. beutiful   B. acrobat   C. perfect   D. balance

25. The armored divizion of the army is expecting to attack at 4:00 a.m.

    A. armored   B. divizion   C. expecting   D. attack

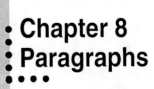

Chapter 8
Paragraphs

This chapter references writing domains
ELA8W1
ELA8W2
ELA8W4

PARAGRAPH STRUCTURE

Well-structured paragraphs are the building blocks of essays, reports, compositions and other writing tasks. You have been writing paragraphs for years, so this section is a brief recap. You probably know the definition of a paragraph: a series of related sentences that make a single point about one subject. This definition contains three important phrases.

Choose one subject:	A paragraph is too brief to discuss more than one subject.
Make a single point:	To "make a point" is to tell readers something that you want them to know. Usually, you will state your point in the topic sentence of your paragraph. The topic sentence often begins a paragraph, though it may also be at the end or in the middle.
Relate other sentences to the topic sentence:	Though you state your point in the topic sentence, you must make your point by providing supporting details. Other sentences in the paragraph provide readers with information and evidence to explain your topic sentence. If the topic sentence does not end the paragraph, a concluding sentence can bring the paragraph to a close, and if appropriate, lead into the next paragraph.

Usually, the **introductory sentence**, which appears at the beginning of the paragraph, presents the main idea. The **concluding sentence**, on the other hand, is a summary of the information in the paragraph and comes at the end of the paragraph. Some paragraphs may contain an **unrelated idea** or **sentence** that does not belong in the paragraph.

Example: 1. The cave's ceiling was covered with jagged stalactites.

2. The cave was a fearsome sight.

3. Bats were flying and squeaking in the cavern.

4. Chet relit the kerosene lantern, bathing the cavern in light.

5. A clown was juggling by the tent.

Logical order in this paragraph: Chet relit the kerosene lantern, bathing the cavern with light. The cave's ceiling was covered with jagged stalactites. Bats were flying and squeaking through the cavern. The cave was a fearsome sight.

Here, **sentence 4** is the **introductory sentence** because it explains what the paragraph describes. **Sentence 2** is the **concluding sentence** because it provides a summary of the action in the paragraph. **Sentence 5**, about the clown, has no place in the description of the cave. That sentence is the **unrelated idea**.

In the next examples, we shall look at sentences describing action:

Example: 1. When we saw the mess she made, we told her "Naughty dog!" and sent her outside.

2. To top it off, she overturned the pot and spilled dirt all over our new carpet.

3. We clipped Bear's paws with gold nail clippers today.

4. Our new puppy, Bear, ruined our potted African violets.

5. As soon as we turned our backs, Bear began eating the violets to the roots.

Logical order in this paragraph: Our new puppy, Bear, ruined our potted African violets. As soon as we turned our backs, Bear began to eat the violets to the roots. To top it off, she overturned the pot and spilled dirt all over our new carpet. When we saw the mess she made, we told her, "Naughty dog!" and sent her outside.

Here, **sentence 4** is the **introductory sentence** because it explains all of the action following it. **Sentence 1** is the **concluding sentence** because it explains the end result of the action. **Sentence 3** is uninvolved in the action of the other sentences, and so, it is the **unrelated idea**. **Sentences 2 and 5** are **supporting sentences**.

Practice 1: Paragraph Structure

In the following exercise, write whether the sentence described is an introductory sentence, concluding sentence, unrelated idea, or supporting sentence.

A. 1. Squawking sea gulls circled above him.

2. The department store had a large neon sign that blinked on and off, lighting the darkness.

3. Mr. Gant sensed he had finally reached the ocean.

4. The smell of saltwater hung thick in the air.

5. He could hear the crashing of the waves.

6. Mr. Gant stopped running through the sand for a moment to check his progress.

Sentence 1_____	Sentence 4_____
Sentence 2_____	Sentence 5_____
Sentence 3_____	Sentence 6_____

B. 1. The facility will destroy a protected wetland environment.

2. The proposed recreational facility is a complete waste of money.

3. My Aunt Sarah doesn't like the man in charge of constructing the facility.

4. Consider the reasons and make the obvious choice to oppose construction of this facility.

5. The county population is not large enough to support its day-to-day operation.

Sentence 1_____	Sentence 4_____
Sentence 2_____	Sentence 5_____
Sentence 3_____	

THE TOPIC SENTENCE OF A PARAGRAPH

You know that a paragraph is organized around a single idea that is stated in the **topic sentence**. The topic sentence tells the reader two important pieces of information:

1) the subject of the paragraph,

2) what the author wants the reader to know about that subject.

As a writer, you can use these statements to help you develop a topic sentence. Begin by answering the following two questions:

What is the subject of the paragraph?

What do I want the reader to know about that subject?

Then use the answers to these questions to form a topic sentence. For example,

Subject: fuel-efficient cars

Want reader to know: help the environment

Sentence: Buying a fuel-efficient car is one way you can help the environment.

This simple method of forming a topic sentence can help you stay focused in your writing. The topic sentence is like your compass while you write. It tells you what direction you want to go. Then, if you feel yourself getting lost in your writing, you can return to your topic sentence to get your bearings. For each sentence in a paragraph, ask the two questions above. If the sentence doesn't relate in some way to the subject and what you want the reader to know about the subject, it doesn't belong in the paragraph.

Practice 2: Writing a Topic Sentence

For each of the following, write a topic sentence based on the subject and what you want the reader to know.

1. Subject: baseball cards

   Want reader to know: it's an interesting hobby

   Topic Sentence: _____

2. Subject: computers in classrooms

   Want reader to know: provide learning opportunities

   Topic Sentence: _____

3. Subject: refugees in the United States

   Want reader to know: struggle without knowledge of English

   Topic Sentence: _____

IMPROVING A TOPIC SENTENCE

The previous exercise may make writing a topic sentence seem easy, but writing a **good topic sentence** is a little more challenging. It is like deciding the best way to begin a conversation. Some people are very good at starting a conversation and keeping it going. They have a talent for inviting others into dialogue by picking a good topic and introducing it in an interesting way.

When you write, you are starting a conversation with the reader. The topic sentence provides the basis for this conversation. A good topic sentence should present *a single idea* that is *broad enough* to *invite discussion*. The three key phrases of this rule are vital to writing a strong topic sentence

1. **Single Idea.** Because a paragraph is focused on one idea, the topic sentence also should be limited to a single idea. Usually, the sentence should have only one subject and one verb.

   Example:

   Incorrect: Baseball players and lawyers get paid too much for the work they do.

This sentence has two subjects: baseball players and lawyers. The support needed for this sentence requires more than one paragraph. Choose one subject for one paragraph.

   Correct: Professional baseball players get paid too much for the work they do.
   OR
   Correct: Lawyers get paid too much for the work they do.

   Example:

   Incorrect: The internet provides computer users with a vast resource of information and creates worldwide marketing opportunities for businesses.

The internet is a single subject, but the sentence describes two services provided by the internet. Either service provides the basis for a good paragraph.

   Correct: The internet provides computer users with a vast resource of information.
   OR
   Correct: The internet creates worldwide marketing opportunities for businesses.

2. **Broad Enough.** The topic sentence must be broad enough so that it can be supported by details. A topic sentence that is really just a detail has no place to go.

Example:

Detail: Baking soda absorbs household odors in carpets and kitchens.

Detail: Lemon juice lightens stains and cuts grease.

Topic: Natural household products can be used for effective cleaning.

The third sentence is broad enough to be supported by the details of the first two sentences. However, the first two sentences are too specific to be discussed in a paragraph. The same is true of the next example.

Example:

Detail: Genetic engineers have succeeded in cloning farm animals.

Detail: Lawyers use DNA tests in criminal court cases.

Topic: In recent years, genetic research has produced astounding, yet practical, results.

3. **Invites Discussion.** A good topic sentence makes the reader want to continue reading. It usually begins the paragraph and should invite the reader to consider the writer's topic.

Example:

Weak: I went to Florida last year.

Good: Florida is the ideal place to go for a winter vacation.

The weak topic sentence doesn't have any energy or movement. There's no clear direction to go in writing, and the reader may not be interested enough to follow. A good topic sentence makes the reader ask questions and want to read more, as in the following two examples.

Example:

Weak: My uncle drives an expensive Italian sports car.

Good: People often choose a particular car as a reflection of their personality.

Practice 3: Choosing a Topic Sentence

For each group of sentences, decide which one could be a good topic sentence. Then explain why the others are not as effective.

1. a. I had never seen so much trash in all my life!
   b. The trash began piling up.
   c. Last summer, I worked for a trash collection company.

2. a. This has been a dry summer.
   b. Rainfall in the metro region is two inches below normal.
   c. This summer's drought may put water supplies in danger.

3. a. Modern rap is rooted in traditional African music.
   b. Modern rap has led to creative innovations in music.
   c. My brother listens to rap music all the time.

ORGANIZATIONAL PATTERNS AND TRANSITIONAL WORDS

Paragraphs need clear organization, and there are many ways to organize paragraphs. Time (**chronological**) **order**, **spatial order**, **order of importance**, **cause and effect**, **comparison**, and **contrast** are some of the most common patterns for organization. By clearly organizing your paragraphs, readers have landmarks or clues as they read that help with comprehension. Imagine getting in an elevator and the buttons for all of the floors are in random order, not numerical order. You would be rather confused and would have to search for the floor number that you need to go to. You expect the numbers to be in some sort of order, largest to smallest and top to bottom, maybe across in rows left to right, or some obvious pattern so you can quickly find the one you need. Organizational patterns in paragraphs are much the same. They help the reader process the information contained in the paragraph.

Within paragraphs, and especially in longer pieces of writing such as essays, **transitional words** are important. It is not enough just to write a series of ideas. You need to lead the reader through your composition by showing how the ideas are related to each other. Transitional words help the reader see the relationship between your ideas. These relationships are based on the organizational patterns mentioned above.

The following sections explain each organizational pattern and give transitional words that can be used to make the relationships between ideas clear to your readers.

USING TRANSITIONAL WORDS

As you write your draft, remember that your reader does not already have a sense of where you are going with your composition. It is not enough for you just to write a series of ideas. You need to lead the reader through your composition by showing how the ideas are related to each other. Transitional words help the reader see the relationship between your ideas. These relationships include chronological order, order of importance, cause and effect, comparison, and contrast.

TIME ORDER

You can use transitional words to show **time order**, that is, when events happen in relation to each other: one event before another, one after another, or both at the same time. Some writers even work with the present and move backwards in time. Read the following example to see what happens when transitional words are missing.

> **Example 1:** *Our family has a daily routine to get us to work and school. My father leaves the house. He wakes up my brother and me. I get up and take a shower. My brother takes a shower. I get dressed. My mother gets our lunches ready. We eat breakfast. We jump in the car and drive to school. Mom drops us off on her way to work.*

Example 1 is choppy because it is missing transitional words to clarify the order of events. Without these words, the reader wonders how the father can leave the house and then wake up his sons. Below is a corrected example with transitional words underlined.

Example 2: *Our family has a daily routine to get us to work and school. <u>Before</u> my father leaves the house, he wakes up my brother and me. I get up <u>first</u> and take a shower. <u>Then</u>, my brother takes a shower <u>while</u> I'm getting dressed. <u>Meanwhile</u>, my mother gets our lunches ready. <u>After</u> breakfast, we jump in the car for the drive to school. <u>Lastly</u>, Mom drops us off on her way to work.*

Using transitional words is a simple and effective way to present your ideas and descriptions clearly. The chart below provides you with examples of transitional words that show chronological order.

Transitional Words for Time Order			
after	again	and then	as
as long as	as soon as	at the same time	before
currently	during	eventually	finally
first	gradually	immediately	in the future
later	meanwhile	now	second
soon	suddenly	then	third
until	when	whenever	while

ORDER OF IMPORTANCE

Transitional words help show which idea you want to emphasize as more important than others. The example below lacks these transitional words.

Example 3: *You should always be aware of your surroundings in parking lots at night. Look over the lot carefully for potential danger spots, for example, areas of low visibility and areas that do not have parking attendants. Be sure you have a defensive weapon, such as pepper spray or a loud noisemaker, in your hand as you walk to your vehicle. Before entering your vehicle, look through the windows to make sure no one is hiding inside.*

Notice how in Example 3 the writer did not use transitional words to indicate whether one of the steps is more important than another. Below is a corrected example with underlined transitional words showing the order of importance.

Example 4: *You should always be aware of your surroundings in parking lots at night. <u>First</u>, look over the lot carefully for potential danger spots, for example, areas of low visibility and areas that do not have parking attendants. <u>More importantly</u>, be sure you have a defensive weapon, such as pepper spray or a loud noisemaker, in your hand as you walk to your vehicle. <u>Above all</u>, before entering your vehicle, look through the windows to make sure no one is hiding inside.*

As you can see, using these transitional words helps to rank the steps required to reduce the potential danger of parking lots at night.

Transitional Words for Order of Importance		
above all	especially	first
in fact	in particular	of highest importance
more importantly	most importantly	

SPATIAL ORDER

When you describe a scene or a location, you can sometimes use **spatial order** to arrange your ideas in a paragraph. Imagine yourself holding a camcorder and moving it in every direction. You can order your observations from **top to bottom**, **left to right**, **clockwise**, **near to far**, **front to back**, **inside to outside**, **east to west**, **north to south**, etc., and all of these directions *reversed* (e.g., **bottom to top**). Read the following description which is organized in spatial order.

When I saw the horse, I knew I was looking at a creature of great athletic beauty and ability. The horse's head was finely shaped, as if sculpted by an artist. On either side of its head, the eyes were alert and far-seeing. The ears were pointed and moved attentively to the slightest sound. The horse's neck was crested in a proud arch, and its muscular shoulders tapered down to powerful legs. The spine of the horse was perfectly aligned, and the back legs were unblemished and moved freely. The hindquarters of the horse were well rounded, and the horse's tail flowed like silk in the wind. In short, this horse was a magnificent animal.

Look at the picture of the horse above. Does it make sense from the description you just read? If not, what additional details or observations would improve the description?

In the passage, the details of the horse are organized in a front to back order. First, the writer discusses the horse's head, along with the eyes and ears. Second, the writer provides details about the neck, shoulders, and front legs. Third, the writer describes the spine and the back legs. Finally, the author tells us about the horse's hindquarters and tail.

Spatial order can also be an effective way to organize other kinds of writing, as you can see in the following example of persuasive writing.

It's time for the city to clean up Jones Park. As visitors enter the park, they are greeted by a broken sign that is smeared with graffiti. Next, they pass the pond where they must hold their noses because of the smell of decaying trash. If visitors make it past all of this, they reach the playground in the middle of the park. Here they find swings with ripped seats hanging limp beside slides with broken steps. The park, in its current state, is a hazardous waste area that must be cleaned up.

Practice 4:   Time Order, Spatial Order, Order of Importance

Look at the pictures below. On a separate sheet of paper, write one paragraph for each picture. Make sure the sentences follow the order listed above the picture.

Time Order	**Spatial Order**	**Order of Importance**

CAUSE AND EFFECT

Linking **causes and effects** is an important aspect of writing a convincing persuasive composition. You can use transitional words to make these connections clear. Read the example below.

Example 5: *Local graffiti "artists" are becoming more brazen. Two weeks ago, they sprayed paint across three community centers. Last week, several businesses found their buildings "decorated" against their wishes. Last night, some graffiti writers took their work inside, painting the twelfth floor of the Baxton Building. The city council announced a special hearing for Thursday of next week to discuss possible responses to this problem.*

The cause and effect relationship in Example 5 is not clear because the paragraph is missing a crucial transition. Read Example 6, and notice how just one transitional phrase (underlined) can bring clarity to this paragraph by signaling the effect of the graffiti writers' activities.

Example 6: *Local graffiti "artists" are becoming more brazen. Two weeks ago, they sprayed paint across three community centers. Last week, several businesses found their buildings "decorated" against their wishes. Last night, some graffiti writers took their work inside to the twelfth floor of the Baxton Building. <u>As a result</u>, the city council announced a special hearing for Thursday of next week to discuss possible responses to this problem.*

Because the writer added one transitional phrase in Example 6, the whole paragraph is clearer. The phrase "as a result" shows that the city council's announcement is an effect of the graffiti writing.

Transitional Words for Cause and Effect				
as a result	because	for this reason	if . . . , then	since
so	so that	therefore	thus	whenever

COMPARISON

Transitional words help a writer show **comparisons**, that is, how certain ideas or subjects are similar. Example 7 lacks these transitions.

Example 7: *The United States and the USSR did not want to enter World War II. They had been forced to enter the fighting because of sneak attacks. The Soviets were caught off guard when Hitler broke his non-aggression treaty and invaded the Soviet Union on June 22, 1941. The United States suffered a surprise attack when the Japanese struck the US naval base at Pearl Harbor on December 7, 1941. From that time on, the two countries were allies in fighting the Axis powers of Germany, Italy, and Japan.*

Due to the lack of transitional words in Example 7, the similarities between the United States' and the Soviet Union's entry into World War II are not as clear as they could be. In fact, the first sentence is awkward. The few well-placed transitions shown in Example 8 make the passage much more effective and easily understood.

Example 8: <u>*Neither*</u> *the United States* <u>*nor*</u> *the USSR had wanted to enter World War II.* <u>*Both*</u> *countries had been forced to enter the fighting because of sneak attacks. The Soviets were caught off guard when Hitler broke his non-aggression treaty and invaded the Soviet Union on June 22, 1941.* <u>*Similarly*</u>*, the United States suffered a surprise attack when the Japanese struck the US naval base at Pearl Harbor on December 7, 1941. From that time on, the two countries were allies in fighting the Axis powers of Germany, Italy, and Japan.*

"Neither" and "nor" may not sound like comparison words, but they point to negative similarity. The other underlined transitional words make the comparisons between the US and the USSR clearer. Also, note the importance of "from that time on" in the last sentence to show the order of events.

Transitional Words for Comparison		
also	as well as	at the same time
both	equally important	in the same way
likewise	neither/nor	similarly

Contrast

Transitional words also help a writer make **contrasts**, or differences, clearer. Read the example below to see how a contrasting paragraph needs transitions.

> **Example 9:** *You may consider caves and mines the same kinds of holes in the ground. They are really quite different. Underground streams and rivers form caves over millions of years through erosion. Humans use machines to dig mines over the course of only a few months. The rapid removal of rock during the mining process requires the use of supports to prevent a mine's ceiling from collapsing. The slow, natural formation of caves makes these supports unnecessary. The slow process of cave formation allows natural gases to escape slowly and safely. Miners must be cautious of the explosive and poisonous gases that are rapidly released as the earth is blasted open. As you can see, human development of the earth is often rapid and dangerous. Nature's development can be gradual and peaceful.*

Example 9 makes sense without transitional words, but it does not flow well. The writer lists ideas but does not connect them. Read Example 10 to see how transitional words can help the flow of the ideas in the paragraph.

> **Example 10:** *You may consider caves and mines the same kinds of holes in the ground, <u>but in reality,</u> they are quite different. Underground streams and rivers form caves over millions of years through erosion. <u>In contrast,</u> humans use machines to dig mines over the course of only a few months. The rapid removal of rock during the mining process requires the use of supports to prevent a mine's ceiling from collapsing. <u>However,</u> the slow, natural formation of caves makes these supports unnecessary. The slow process of cave formation <u>also</u> allows natural gases to escape slowly and safely, <u>whereas</u> miners must be cautious of the explosive and poisonous gases that are rapidly released as the earth is blasted open. As you can see, human development of the earth is often rapid and dangerous, <u>while</u> nature's development can be gradual and peaceful.*

Transitional Words for Contrast

although	and yet	but	despite
even so	even	though	however
in contrast	instead of	in spite of	nevertheless
on the one hand	on the other hand	rather than	still
whereas	while		

Tip
Use transitional words to help the reader see the relationship between your ideas. These relationships include chronological order, order of importance, cause and effect, comparison, and contrast.

UNRELATED SENTENCES

Once you have decided on an organizational pattern, you want to be sure that you are consistent with it. After a few sentences, the reader begins to expect a certain pattern, and it can be very confusing if some sentences don't follow the pattern. You have probably experienced someone telling about a movie or book and they kept saying, "Oh, but back before that so and so happened." It is very hard to keep track of what they are telling you if they jump around and you are expecting them to tell the story in order from beginning to end.

When you revise and edit your own writing, keep in mind the organizational pattern you are using and then look for sentences that are out of order or sequence. Try to put yourself in the reader's position and think about what previous information is required to understand each point you are making. If that previous information doesn't appear before your point, the reader doesn't have the background he or she needs.

In some cases, you may want or need to add information, ideas, or examples to your sentences. In other cases, you will want to eliminate information, ideas, or examples if they do not relate directly to the topic of your essay. Again, putting yourself in the reader's position will help you realize if something is missing, or if there is extra information that the reader doesn't need.

Practice 5: Deleting Unrelated Sentences

Read each of the following paragraphs, and draw a line through the unrelated sentence.

1. Out of all the classes you take in high school, not one of them deals with real-life situations. For example, you can get your diploma and not once have you been taught how to apply for college admission or for a full-time job. It seems like no one knows what's going on! Also, nobody has taught you how to communicate effectively or what skills are necessary in the interview process. Even if you get a job or go to college, no one has taught you how to get a checking account, apply for a lease, or even file your federal and state tax returns. It's a wonder any of us can make it to adulthood given our lack of education!

2. My first day in high school was pretty challenging. For the first time, I changed to a different class every fifty minutes. The school was huge, and I got lost during every move. I showed up to every class late. To top it all off, the combination to my locker didn't work, so I had to carry all of my books the entire day. I was not looking forward to going home, either, because I had to mow the lawn. My only consolation was that the other students in my classes were really friendly, and the teachers were understanding of what happens that first day.

3. When Leah turned the corner and entered the perfume shop at the mall, she got more than she bargained for. The most horrid smell in the world assaulted her nose. Customers

and sales associates in this store were coughing and gagging! Leah pinched her nose quickly and ran for her life. After running for about fifty feet with her nose pinched, she released her nose and breathed some fresh air. There's nothing like fresh air to increase your mental functioning. After that incident, Leah thought it would be best to go home. Then, the next morning, she read about someone placing a stink bomb in the store as a prank.

4.   I look forward to a solution to the problem of the super-sensitive security motion sensor. Once that type of motion sensor is activated, the slightest movement can set it off. A flying moth or even my cat scratching the litter box after a large dinner can send loud sounds pulsating through my house. I know the sensor needs to detect the sounds and motions of a thief, but how many thieves are actually as small as a moth or as silent as a cat? A home security system is very expensive.

Practice 6: Organizational Patterns and Transitional Words

Read the paragraphs below. Decide how each paragraph seems to be organized, whether by time order, spatial order, order of importance, cause and effect, comparison, or contrast. Then, rewrite the paragraph on a separate sheet of paper, adding appropriate transitional words or phrases.

1.   There are many things to remember as you get ready to go back to school. Develop a positive attitude about the upcoming school year. Make sure you understand your class schedule. You know your classes. You should buy plenty of school supplies such as pens, paper, notebooks, and a calculator. Take time to inventory your clothes, and make sure you have the clothes you need. These tasks are completed. You will be ready for the new school year.

2.   Both your beliefs and your actions are important in leading an exemplary life. Your beliefs should guide you to knowing how to act in all situations. If your actions do not match what you believe, people will not listen to what you say. If you act in a way that seems good to others, but you have no beliefs to explain your actions, people may label you as shallow. Be certain and careful with both your beliefs and your actions in order to be an example to others.

3.   The preparation required for a test is quite similar to the preparation needed for a sports event. Training for any sports event requires daily practice to keep the athlete's body in good condition. Test preparation requires daily practice and review to keep the scholar's memory up to date. The night before a sporting event, the athlete must get plenty of rest. A scholar must rest his or her mind, so it will be fresh for the big event of the test. A good athlete will take pride in a nutritious diet that provides the building blocks for a strong body. A scholar must feed the mind with nutritious food to increase mental skill. Test-taking may not have the same glamour as athletic competition, but both activities require preparation in order to achieve success.

SUPPORTING SENTENCES

Just as the Academy Awards has a category for Best Supporting Actor, some sentences and information are better choices than others for supporting a paragraph topic. Choosing supporting information for a paragraph is a matter of judgement. The judgement has to be made with consideration to the particular topic, audience, purpose, and information available.

In choosing supporting information, ask yourself, "Which information gives the strongest support for the topic?" Also consider the audience, "Which support information will make the biggest impression on my intended audience?" Supporting facts or information that would convince or impress your parents is probably not the same information that would convince or impress your classmates.

When choosing information and details for a paragraph, also take into consideration the purpose of your writing. A large number of descriptive details may not be necessary for writing that is primarily meant to be persuasive, and so on.

Practice 7: Supporting Sentences

For each of the following short paragraphs, choose the additional sentence that would be the best additional support to the paragraph.

1.   My fellow students: We have got to do something about the litter and trash problem here on campus. We are all old enough to know that we need to pick up after ourselves. I see students dropping empty drink bottles in the shrubbery around the cafeteria. In the out-side lunch area, some people leave all their trash on the table and just walk away. The first wind that comes along blows it all over the lawn area.

   A.   The trash problems around here are becoming overwhelming.
   B.   None of us has a personal servant following behind us.
   C.   Last week I saw two rats eating near the picnic tables.
   D.   The March winds will turn your umbrella inside out.

2.   **My Attitude**

        I have come to know that nothing can make or break my day more than my attitude. It is more important than what I'm wearing today, what I'm going to eat for lunch, or how my hair turned out. I've learned when I smile at people, they smile back. When I'm touchy or grouchy, people back away from me. When I'm upset, concentrating on being positive can turn my day around.

   A.   Most of what happens to me on any given day depends upon my attitude.
   B.   Sesame Street's Oscar has a bad attitude.
   C.   Rap stars often express attitude.
   D.   A bad attitude can get you fired.

CONCLUDING SENTENCES

The concluding sentence of a paragraph brings closure to the paragraph by providing a summary of the topic and the supporting details. It may also suggest what action the reader should take, especially in persuasive writing. If another paragraph follows, the concluding sentence serves as a link between the two paragraphs.

A paragraph that lacks a concluding sentence may leave the reader hanging, as if in midair, wondering if the author left out something. Read the example below to understand the importance of concluding sentences.

> **Example:** The federal government should increase spending for defense. Now that the war on terrorism has started, there is a need to keep this country well-armed. Currently, the United States spends more for defense than all other countries in the world combined! Congress continues to approve larger amounts of money for defense.

This paragraph lacks an ending. The paragraph begins with an opinion about the amount of money spent for defense, and supporting details follow to back up this point. However, the lack of a conclusion leaves the reader wondering whether the paragraph is finished.

The addition of a concluding sentence like the following would make a big difference.

Concluding Sentence:

> *Write to your representatives to say the terrorist attacks have justified every penny spent on defense and more.*

This one sentence ties the paragraph together by summarizing the main idea and supporting details and urging the reader to take action. The reader may agree or disagree with the writer's ideas, but the reader has no doubt that the writer has brought the paragraph to a close.

Practice 8: Concluding Sentences

Read the following paragraphs, and write a concluding sentence that best completes the topic. If the paragraph has a concluding sentence, write **correct**.

1.   The global economy is moving toward the East. By 2020, China is projected to have an economy that is roughly eleven times as large as the economy of the United States! In addition, Japan, India, and Indonesia will have production levels that rival the United States. Only four nations in Europe will even make the top twenty list of the world's largest economies.

2.   The dancing craze is back in full force in the United States. After years of obscurity, swing music and dancing have made a rapid comeback. Also, the Latin rhythms of salsa, merengue, and cumbia can be heard in many cities. Two-stepping in clubs playing country music is also popular. In addition, the clubs playing techno, hip hop, and R&B music continue to draw larger crowds.

3.   Lifting weights is both mentally and physically demanding. It takes a great amount of concentration to lift large weights safely. Every lifter knows that form is crucial. The lifter must understand and visualize what he or she is doing during every second of a lift. People who do not exercise their mind in this manner end up with strains, sprains, and back and neck injuries.

POINT OF VIEW

A story's **point of view** is the perspective, or outlook, from which a the story is told. There may be a character narrating the story, or there may be an unidentified speaker describing the action and thoughts of all main characters. For example, Mary Shelley writes *Frankenstein* from the first person point of view, but she uses three different narrators to tell their own stories: Dr. Frankenstein, the creator of the monster; the monster himself; and Walton, the last man to speak to both.

THREE TYPES OF POINT OF VIEW

First Person	In the **first person**, a narrator tells the story from the "I" point of view. In *The House On Mango Street*, Esperanza tells her story as the main character. Likewise, in *Shiloh*, Marty Preston, the main character, narrates the story about himself and a dog.
Second Person	In the **second person**, the speaker is talking to you and uses the pronoun "you." This is not often used on its own, but the second person reference is fairly common in poetry, short essays, and songs. For example, the songs "You Are My Sunshine" and "You've Got a Friend."
Third Person	The speaker tells a story describing characters as "he," "she," or "they" as in *The Pearl* by John Steinbeck.
• **omniscient**	Omniscient means "all-knowing." In the **third person omniscient**, the narrator is capable of knowing, telling, and seeing all that happens to the main characters. In Guy de Maupassant's "The Necklace," the third person speaker describes all the story action and the inner thoughts of the main characters.
• **limited**	In the **third person limited** point of view, the speaker tells the story knowing only what is seen, heard, and felt by the thoughts and viewpoint of one character, usually the main character. In Crane's *Red Badge of Courage*, the author tells the story through the soldier, Henry. We experience the events through Henry's eyes and ears.

Deciding what point of view the author is using to tell a story is a first big step in understanding how that story will work. When you determine what the point of view is, you are ahead in understanding how the frame for the story will be set.

The choice of narrator affects the **credibility of a text**. The credibility of a text simply means how believable the story is for the reader. Is the voice true to the character, the place of the story, and the time of the story? If the answer to these questions is yes, then the voice helps the story become believable to the reader. One example of a credible text is Phyllis Reynold's *Shiloh*. Naylor's narrator is a boy whose voice reflects the time and place of the story.

A first person narrator who is very honest and clear-sighted, such as Naylor's Marty, may be well trusted in telling a story. This point of view, however, is limited to the narrator's experience and feelings only. The same holds true for the limited third person. For example, in Stephen Crane's *The Red Badge of Courage*, only one character, the young soldier, is understood completely. The third person omniscient is the most knowing position for a narrator. However, does this narrator simply give the facts and details to the reader and let the reader make decisions about the story, or does the narrator state an opinion and expect the reader to agree? A believable narrator will let readers decide what they think about a story. An example of this type of narration is John Steinbeck's novel *Of Mice and Men*.

SENTENCE ERRORS

As you learned in chapters 6and o1 of this book, errors within a paragraph are common. In the following example, check the sentences for errors in punctuation, capitalization, and spelling.

Example: 1. Nathan and John drove North of Birmingham to fish in Wheeler Lake.

2. They stopped at a bait and tackle shop bought some lures and drove to the lake.

3. Together, they caught one dosen fish in the lake.

4. They cleaned the fish at home and had a feast.

In this example, **sentence 1** contains a **capitalization error** (north, not North), **sentence 2** contains a **punctuation error** (add commas - items in a series), and **sentence 3** contains a **spelling error** (dozen, not dosen). **Sentence 4** has **no errors**.

Practice 9: Sentence Errors

In the following exercise, tell whether the sentences contain errors in punctuation, capitalization, spelling, or no error.

A. 1. Stacy and Gina were having a difficult time with their algebra I homework.

2. Together, they arranged to hire a tutor.

3. The tutor showed them step-by-step how to correctly answer the   problems

4. On their next examination, both students received A's.

Sentence 1_____Sentence 2_____

Sentence 3_____Sentence 4_____

B. 1. Niko and Kathy went to turkey for their honeymoon.

2. They had a great view of the ancient city of Ephesus from they're hotel room.

3. In the afternoon they enjoyed surfing in the Mediterranean Sea.

4. They usually went dancing at the surrounding nightclubs after dinner.

Sentence 1_____Sentence 2_____

Sentence 3_____Sentence 4_____

Grammatical errors within a paragraph are common. In the following examples, check the sentences for errors in usage.

Example: 1. When I was a little kid, I want to grow up to be a police officer.

2. Now that I am older, I knows I want to do that.

3. Their're needed and receive respect.

4. They put themself in danger everday and keep streets safely.

5. I sure don't want no job except to be a police officer.

In this example, **sentence 1** contains a **verb tense error** (wanted, not want), **sentence 2** contains a **subject-verb agreement error** (know, not knows), and **sentence 3** contains a **homonym error** (they're, not their're). **Sentence 4** has **three errors.** The first is a **pronoun error** (themselves, not themself). The second error is a **spelling** error (everyday, not everday). The third error is a **word form error** (safe, not safely). Sentence 5 has a **double negative** error (any instead of no). It also has a word form error (**surely, not sure**).

Practice 10: Grammatical Errors

Read the following sentences. Write the type of grammatical error each sentence contains on the blanks provided. If a sentence does not have a grammatical error, write C in the blank.

A. 1. When I was in the seventh grade, I would tell people I was going to be a professional football player when I growed up.

2. When I got to high school, I didt even make the team.

3. My dream was shattered; my self-esteem gone.

4. Then my uncle had talk with me.

5. He made me sees my other talents like how good I am working with my hands.

6. Now I'm lookin at myself with respect again and checking out other career choices.

Sentence 1 _____ Sentence 4 _____

Sentence 2 _____ Sentence 5 _____

Sentence 3 _____ Sentence 6 _____

B. 1. Sylvia's desire work with horses is fed by a deep love for these creatures.

2. She is captivated by its beauty, strength, and spirit.

3. After leasing one horse for several months, Sylvia grows very attached to him.

4. The horse, Beauty, taught Sylvia that horses have deep relationships with others, even humans.

5. That relationship has continued to impress me and others for years.

Sentence 1 _____ Sentence 4 _____

Sentence 2 _____ Sentence 5 _____

Sentence 3 _____

As you know, run-ons and sentence fragments are very easy errors to make when writing. Read the following sentences and identify whether the sentence is a *run-on*, *fragment*, or *correct.*

Example: 1. One of the things I'm thankful for is the coaching I had taking gymnastics.

2. Being a positive person that easy for me.

3. Gymnastics taught me if I could not do something I had to get up and try again, I had to be positive and tell myself I could do it, I learned to prove to myself I could do it.

4. It kept me on my feet, it taught me I could do anything with my life.

In this example, sentence 1 is **correct.** Sentence 2 is a **fragment** because **that easy for me** is not a complete sentence and neither is **being a positive person**. Sentence 3 is a **run-on** because it has three simple sentences inside of it that have been joined by commas. Sentence 4 is a **run-on** because there are two complete sentences joined by a comma without a conjunction.

Practice 11: Run-ons

Run-ons and fragments are common errors within a paragraph. In the following exercises, check the sentences for run-ons and fragments. Write C if the sentence is correct.

A. 1. The most important ambition in my life right now is to start playing soccer again I miss the game so much it is all I can think about.

2. I played for eight years before being injured.

3. I miss being out on the field at 7 a.m.

4. The smell of the air.

5. The fog lifting from the ground.

6. The blue tint to everything is just a beautiful sight to behold.

Sentence 1 _____ Sentence 4 _____

Sentence 2 _____ Sentence 5 _____

Sentence 3 _____ Sentence 6 _____

B. 1. I want to go back to playing soccer.

2. To feel the anticipation before a game.

3. The Adrenaline rush.

4. There is nothing like it.

5. Somehow I must find the time to play the game I love so much the tournaments are so exciting.

Sentence 1 _____ Sentence 4 _____

Sentence 2 _____ Sentence 5 _____

Sentence 3 _____

CHAPTER 8 REVIEW

All of the sentences except one in each series make a paragraph. Write I if the sentence is introductory, S if the sentence is supporting, C if the sentence is concluding, and U if the sentence is an unrelated idea.

1. 1. Roy Garston was playing Hacky Sack™ with his friends.

2. One guy bounced the sack six times on his feet.

3. Gina Molina ran the mile in under seven minutes.

4. Brad and Alex did some amazing back kicks with the Hacky Sack™.

5. The Hacky Sack™ provided hours of enjoyment for everyone playing.

Sentence 1 _____ Sentence 3 _____ Sentence 5 _____

Sentence 2 _____ Sentence 4 _____

2. 1. Jessica always slammed the volleyball as hard as she could.

2. Carrie took the day off and visited the zoo.

3. The volleyball game was just beginning.

4. This was going to be a very exciting game.

5. Polly and Amanda loved to return the ball spinning across the net.

Sentence 1 _____ Sentence 3 _____ Sentence 5 _____

Sentence 2 _____ Sentence 4 _____

3. 1. The Bug Be Gone Company sprayed with pesticides every year.

2. The last alternative at this time seems to be raising chickens around the school campus.

3. School officials were puzzled as to how they could get rid of their black widow spiders.

4. Then a black widow spider bit a teacher twice.

5. Before pesticides, farmers raised chickens to keep the spider population down.

6. Littering is a constant problem on the school grounds.

Sentence 1 _____ Sentence 3 _____ Sentence 5 _____

Sentence 2 _____ Sentence 4 _____ Sentence 6 _____

4. 1. Science and experience show that a meatless diet can increase athletic performance.

2. Many leading athletes are switching to vegetarian diets for the benefits they receive.

3. Scientists know that the body can process complex carbohydrates easier than fats and proteins.

4. Better exercise programs have helped increase athletic performance.

5. Remember, fresh fruits, vegetables, and grains are the keys to a healthy athlete's diet.

Sentence 1 _____ Sentence 3 _____ Sentence 5 _____

Sentence 2 _____ Sentence 4 _____

5. 1. All of the cafeteria workers were dressed in traditional Hawaiian clothes.

2. Mrs. Chessner drove a pickup truck to school.

3. Today was Hawaiian luau day at the school cafeteria.

4. This was the best lunch day of the year for us.

5. The principal gave us Hawaiian leis made out of orchids to wear.

6. We ate fresh pineapple and grilled pork for lunch.

Sentence 1 _____ Sentence 3 _____ Sentence 5 _____

Sentence 2 _____ Sentence 4 _____ Sentence 6 _____

6. 1. Guinea pigs are great companions for young children.

2. Hamsters are great fun to be with and make cute friends, too!

3. When you feed a hamster, it will stuff its food in its cheeks.

4. They love to explore and exercise in spinning wheels.

5. Hamsters are very interesting pets to own.

Sentence 1 _____ Sentence 3 _____ Sentence 5 _____

Sentence 2 _____ Sentence 4 _____

Read the following sentence groups and identify which sentences contain errors. Write S if the sentence contains a spelling error, C if the sentence contains a capitalization error, P if the sentence contains a punctuation error, and N if the sentence does not contain an error.

7. 1. Chelsea calmed herself as she approacht the uneven bars.

2. She quickly jumped on the bottom beam and began her routine

3. The whirling motion of chealsea's body made the crowd dizzy with excitement.

4. She landed perfectly on the mat on her dismount.

5. The crowd rose to its feet and upplauded for five minutes.

Sentence 1 _____ Sentence 3 _____ Sentence 5 _____

Sentence 2 _____ Sentence 4 _____

8. 1. George and Carrie started to play a video game called *galaxy wars*.

2. The object of the game was to battle the evil forces of Typhos and to free imprisoned worlds.

3. Both George and Carrie fought off the opposing space ships four three hours.

4. In the end they defeated the game and freed the planets from the power of Typhos.

5. They celebrated by eating thirdy chocolate chip cookies.

Sentence 1 _____ Sentence 3 _____ Sentence 5 _____

Sentence 2 _____ Sentence 4 _____

9. 1. Scarlett and Hogan spent two days listening to their favrite alternative band, *Broken Glass.*

2. They spent three hours writing to the fan club, asking for ways to contact the band members.

3. with their hard-earned allowance money, they bought life-size posters of the members of *Broken Glass.*

4. Both Scarlett and Hogan wrote the lyrics from the bands songs on their book bags.

5. All of their friends thought that Scarlett and Hogan should seek professional counseling.

Sentence 1 _____ Sentence 3 _____ Sentence 5 _____

Sentence 2 _____ Sentence 4 _____

10. 1. Trudi started the lawn mower with her friends help.

2. She started mowing and accidentally ran over a big, squishy rhinoceros beetle.

3. "EEK!" she cried as the bug juices splattered her tennis shoe.

4. Trudi ran in the house took off her shoes and cleaned them with a toothbrush.

5. The next morning, Trudi forgot what happened and used the same toothbrush for her teeth.

Sentence 1 _____ Sentence 3 _____ Sentence 5 _____

Sentence 2 _____ Sentence 4 _____

11. 1. Jordan took a trip to the beach with his cousin, Hope.

2. While they were walking along the beach a crab clamped onto Hope's foot.

3. Jordan tried to get the crab off of Hope's foot, but it would not release Hope's toe.

4. In desperation, Jordan screamed at the crab "Get off my friend, or I'll eat you for supper!"

5. The crab released Hope and scuttled away to look for a fish dinner.

Sentence 1 _____ Sentence 3 _____ Sentence 5 _____

Sentence 2 _____ Sentence 4 _____

Read the following sentence groups, and check each sentence for grammatical errors. Write P if there is a pronoun error, T if there is an error in verb tense, V if there is a subject-verb agreement error, D if there is a double negative error, and PO if there is an error in making nouns or pronouns possessive.

12. 1. Lucinda and her friend, Yin, ridden their bikes through the busy streets.

2. Everywhere they went, they threw candy at the children they see.

3. The children would fights each other for the candy.

4. Lucinda's face glowed when she saw the smiles on the children's face.

5. After the long day was through, Yin and Lucinda didn't ride their bikes nowhere.

Sentence 1 _____ Sentence 3 _____ Sentence 5 _____

Sentence 2 _____ Sentence 4 _____

13. 1. An ambition of myself is becoming involved in a career that allows me to work with computers.

2. I enjoy use computers in my everyday life, in my education, and in my small home business.

3. In my spare time, I tinker with my computer, exploring functions of the various software and hardware in an effort to understand how it works.

4. I am also not hardly uncomfortable using computers and can learn tasks on them quickly.

5. I believe that a person should enjoy his or her work, so they would be perfect for me.

Sentence 1 _____ Sentence 3 _____ Sentence 5 _____

Sentence 2 _____ Sentence 4 _____

Read the following sentences. Write R if the sentence is a run-on, F if the sentence is a fragment, and C if the sentence is correct.

14. 1. One of my ambitions is to lose fifty pounds.

2. I have faith in myself because I have done it before, I eat low fat meals and I exercise.

3. I know in my heart I need the drive and the patience to make it happen.

4. My mom helps and supports me by going through my diet plan with me.

5. Buying low-fat food at the store.

6. I'm feeling healthier every day I think I will lose the weight.

Sentence 1 _____ Sentence 3 _____ Sentence 5 _____

Sentence 2 _____ Sentence 4 _____ Sentence 6 _____

15. 1. My ambition is to own my own business so I can help my community in some way.

2. I don't like to see my community doing badly I want the people to know someone cares.

3. Ambition is like a chain reaction.

4. When one has it.

5. It passes on to others like wildfire.

6. People will see my community spirit they will want to help out, too.

Sentence 1 _____ Sentence 3 _____ Sentence 5 _____

Sentence 2 _____ Sentence 4 _____ Sentence 6 _____

CHAPTER 8 TEST

Select the best answer for each question.

Four of the five sentences in the box below make a paragraph. Read the sentences. Then answer the questions below the box.

---

1. Her arms swayed back and forth like willow trees in the breeze.
2. Carrie's performance was exceptional at the ballet.
3. This was Carrie's best performance of the season.
4. Donavan did a very good job with the scenery.
5. She never missed a step in her dance movements.

---

1. Which sentence is the best concluding sentence?
   A. Sentence 1   B. Sentence 2   C. Sentence 3   D. Sentence 5

2. Which sentence contains an unrelated idea?
   A. Sentence 1   B. Sentence 3   C. Sentence 4   D. Sentence 5

---

1. This eruption preserved and hid the city of Pompeii for over 1,500 years.
2. The volcanoes of the Hawaiian Islands are very spectacular.
3. The ashes from the eruption covered the entire city.
4. Poisonous gas from the eruption killed most of the people of Pompeii within minutes.
5. Mt. Vesuvius erupted, sentencing the citizens of Pompeii to immediate death.

---

3. Which sentence is the best introductory sentence?
   A. Sentence 1   B. Sentence 4   C. Sentence 3   D. Sentence 5

4. Which sentence is the best concluding sentence?
   A. Sentence 1   B. Sentence 4   C. Sentence 2   D. Sentence 5

---

1. The routine of a caravan on the march is as changeless as the desert itself.
2. The morning begins as a walk through the desert before the temperature is too hot.
3. In the afternoon, the Bedouins mount their camels and spare their bodies from overheating.
4. Nature has made sure this routine will not change for many years to come.
5. The tropical rain forest can reach high temperatures in the afternoon.

---

5. Which sentence contains an unrelated idea?

    A.   Sentence 1   B.   Sentence 2   C.   Sentence 4   D.   Sentence 5

6. Which sentence is the best concluding sentence?

    A.   Sentence 1   B.   Sentence 3   C.   Sentence 4   D.   Sentence 5

---

1. The lake had been recently stocked with trout.
2. That summer day in July was perfect for jet skiing.
3. Everyone who rode the jet skis had a really great time.
4. The wind was strong which increased the size of the waves.
5. The water was warm which made falling in it a pleasant experience

---

7. Which sentence is the best introductory sentence?

    A.   Sentence 1   B.   Sentence 2   C.   Sentence 3   D.   Sentence 4

8. Which sentence is the best concluding sentence?

    A.   Sentence 2   B.   Sentence 3   C.   Sentence 4   D.   Sentence 5

---

1. Everyone on both teams was completely focused on winning because the rivalry between the schools was so serious.
2. The basketball game was very intense.
3. My brother was on my team which made us even more competitive on the court.
4. Our football team made three touchdowns during the entire year.
5. The fans would remember this game as the most exciting of the season.

---

9. Which sentence contains an unrelated idea?

    A.   Sentence 1   B.   Sentence 2   C.   Sentence 3   D.   Sentence 4

10. Which sentence is the best concluding sentence?

    A.   Sentence 1   B.   Sentence 32   C.   Sentence 3   D.   Sentence 5

Read each sentence for a possible error in punctuation, capitalization, or spelling. Select the correct answer.

---

1. Ronald Kaspar was leading our snorkeling expedition off the coast of Key West.
2. All of us were excited about exploring the colorful fish and corals underneath the sea.
3. Our tour guide gave us detailed instructions about what to look for in the reef.
4. All of us were surprised to find Barracuda in the water.

---

11. In sentence 2, there is

    A. an error in punctuation.
    B. a misspelled word.
    C. an error in capitalization.
    D. no error.

12. In sentence 4, there is

    A. an error in punctuation.
    B. a misspelled word.
    C. an error in capitalization.
    D. no error.

---

1. Chad and Shep decided they were going to meet their friends in the grocery store parking lot after school.

2. They held a contest among all their friends to see who had the best sounding stereo system in their vehicle.

3. Each contestant turned on his or her stereo, and the rest graded the sound on tone quality base output and volume range.

4. Chad's refinished 1969 Ford Mustang™ had the best sound system.

---

13. In sentence 1, there is

    A. an error in punctuation.
    B. a misspelled word.
    C. an error in capitalization.
    D. no error.

14. In sentence 3, there is

    A. an error in punctuation.
    B. a misspelled word.
    C. an error in capitalization.
    D. no error.

---

1. Kelly and Trina were running through the school, trying to make it to band practice before it started.

2. Trina slipped on the slick floor and flew headlong into the back of Kelly.

3. Kelly slammed into the floor with her knees and hands, injuring her left knee and fracturing both wrists.

4. Kelly went to the hospital instead of practicing with mr. Stern, her band director.

---

15. In sentence 2, there is

    A. an error in punctuation.
    B. a misspelled word.
    C. an error in capitalization.
    D. no error.

16. In sentence 4, there is

    A. an error in punctuation.
    B. a misspelled word.
    C. an error in capitalization.
    D. no error.

1. Rhoda was sitting with her friends when her beeper began sounding in the restaraunt.

2. The number displayed on the pager was unfamiliar to Rhoda but was followed by 911.

3. While she went to use the phone, her friends brought out her birthday cake and gifts.

4. after calling a wrong number, Rhoda returned to the table and was completely surprised.

17. In sentence 1, there is

    A.   an error in punctuation.

    B.   an error in capitalization.

    C.   a missspelled word.

    D.   no error.

18. In sentence 4, there is

    A.   an error in punctuation.

    B.   an error in capitalization.

    C.   a missspelled word.

    D.   no error.

1. Mark, David, and James drove to the local arcade, which was inside the mall.

2. Here were their favorite games "Killer Instinct," Galaga," and "Teenage Mutant Ninja Turtles."

3. All three of them decided to play "Teenage Mutant Ninja Turtles" since two kids were playing the other two games.

4. They enjoyed the game so much the arcade custodian had to ask them to leave when the mall closed.

19. In sentence 2, there is

    A.   an error in punctuation.

    B.   a misspelled word.

    C.   an error in capitalization.

    D.   no error.

20. In sentence 3, there is

    A.   an error in punctuation.

    B.   a misspelled word.

    C.   an error in capitalizatio.

    D.   no error.

Read the following sentences. Decide whether the sentence has a certain type of grammatical error or whether the sentence is correct. Circle the best answer.

21. I found out I didn't never want to do that again.

    A.   double negative error

    B.   error in possessive case

    C.   pronoun-antecedent agreement error

    D.   no error

22. The coats belonged to she and I.

    A.   verb tense error

    B.   double negative error

    C.   error in possessive case

    D.   no error

23. Your three friends seems to be enjoying themselves at the baseball game.

    A.   pronoun-antecedent agreement error   C.   error in possessive case

    B.   subject-verb agreement error   D.   double negative error

24. When the company develops a new motion picture, all of Hollywood was surprised.

    A.   double negative error   C.   subject-verb agreement error

    B.   verb tense error   D.   pronoun-antecedent agreement error

25. Being in the country restored him sense of purpose.

    A.   error in possessive case   C.   verb tense error

    B.   double negative error   D.   pronoun-antecedent agreement error

Read the following sentences. Decide whether the sentence is a *fragment, run-on,* or *complete sentence*.

26. Looking in the hole were bees everywhere.

    A.   sentence fragment   B.   run-on   C.   complete sentence

27. Giving of yourself is one of the most rewarding things a person can do.

    A.   sentence fragment   B.   run-on   C.   complete sentence

28. The best stories in life come from personal experience, there is no better way to write.

    A.   sentence fragment   B.   run-on   C.   complete sentence

29. Many are called, but few are chosen.

    A.   sentence fragment   B.   run-on   C.   complete sentence

30. Up the hill and through the valley.

    A.   sentence fragment   B.   run-on   C.   complete sentence

Chapter 9
Using Resource Materials

This chapter references writing domain	
	ELA8W2

If you were thinking about getting running shoes, where would you buy them and how much would you pay? If you're a smart shopper, you would browse through the newspaper ads for a shoe sale. Or you might scan the phone directory. Then you might call some stores near you to check prices and shoe sizes available. If you decided to shop at a mall or shopping center, you'd probably look over the mall directory, so you could find the shoe stores that carry the brand you want.

The ability to choose and use reference sources is an essential life skill in today's society. Whether you are buying shoes, doing research in the library, or reading a schedule or diagram, you will face situations where you will need the right resources. Obtaining and using the information from these sources can help you answer questions or complete a task in school, at home, or on the job.

LEARNING AND USING REFERENCE SOURCES

In this part of the chapter, you'll learn about important reference sources. You'll also practice answering questions about these sources. Here are the main ones:

Alphabetizing   Encyclopedia

Thesaurus   Internet and Databases

Almanacs and Magazines   Newspaper Index

Sections of a Book   Newspaper Ad
- Table of Contents
- Index
- Bibliography
- Glossary

At the end of this chapter you will find tips that will help you choose which reference source is right for your current task.

ALPHABETIZING

When lists of words are organized in some manner, the most common method of organization is **alphabetical order**. When words are alphabetized, they are arranged from the letters A – Z in the alphabet.

Many times, words in alphabetical order will begin with the same letter. In these cases, use the second letter of the word to decide which will go first. If the second letter is also the same letter, use the third letter, etc.

Example: **r**aw - first letter   l**e**mon - second letter   Har**d**ing - third letter
         sail   l**o**an   Has**c**al

All reference sources list their topics by alphabetical order. Telephone books and dictionaries post two guide words at the top of each page. Any entry can be found by simply looking for the entry between the guide words.

Example: <u>Realtors - Temporary</u> are guide words. <u>Telephone</u> is a word you could find on that page.

Other reference sources alphabetize by putting the first letter of the volume or drawer in which you will find all words starting with that letter or letters. Encyclopedias and card catalogs use this system.

Example: The letters <u>N - O</u> are listed on the front of a card catalog drawer. The subject <u>oriental</u> an be found in this drawer.

One reference source, the directory, alphabetizes by putting the last names of persons or the names of companies on a large sign. The names are placed in alphabetical order from top to bottom.

Example:	**Room Number**
Atley and Company	106
Durham Foundation	210
Hands On Office Products	113
Lip Saver Technologies	302
Narcotics Recovery Counseling Service	111
Penn & Schuman Message Center	205
Vibrant Voices, Inc.	303

NOTE: If you wanted to add *Car Care, Inc.* to the directory, it would have to be placed between *Atley & Co.* and *Durham Foundation.*

Practice 1: Alphabetizing

Select the correct answer.

1. If you are looking for the entry *aggravation* in the dictionary, which words could you find at the top of the page?

   A.   afraid – against   C.   aflame – agrarian

   B.   agriculture – ajar   D.   agree – amount

Arts and Sciences Building

Office Number

Dr. Greg Ainsley	105
Dr. Vicky Greene	206
Dr. Steve Loxley	203
Dr. Richard Planter	312
Dr. Laura Shannon	113
Dr. George Tinley	109
Dr. Sarah Vanderbilt	308

2. Dr. Zell Manford, a new faculty member in the Arts & Sciences Building, will have his name added to the above alphabetized building directory between
   A. Dr. Steve Loxley and Dr. Richard Planter.
   B. Dr. Richard Planter and Dr. Laura Shannon.
   C. Dr. Vicky Greene and Dr. Steve Loxley.
   D. Dr. Greg Ainsley and Dr. Vicky Greene.

3. If you are looking through the card catalog for the word *zoology*, which drawer would you look in to find the card?
   A. A   B. W – Z   C. N – O   D. Q – R

4. If the guide words *Furniture - Garage* were at the top of a page in the yellow pages, which listing could be included on that page?
   A. Flooring   B. Fender Repair   C. Garbage Collection   D. Futons

5. If you were looking for the word *roundhouse* in the dictionary, which words would you find at the top of the page?
   A. roar – runt   B. ranch – rill   C. rat – roadhouse   D. rouse – rust

6. If you are looking in the *J – K* encyclopedia, which of the following articles will you find?
   A. Catholicism   B. Indiana   C. Lithuania   D. Jakarta

7. If you are looking for the name *Gulianni* in the white pages of the telephone book, which guide words could be listed at the top of the page?
   A. Guthrie – Gylord
   B. Goethe – Gusman
   C. Goodrum – Guff
   D. Gunther – Guy

Atwater National Bank	Suite No
Ms Nancy Birch	524
Mr. Phillip Dorman	213
Mrs. Gail Keckley	406
Ms Monique Givens	106
Mr. Randall Landover	301
Mr. Jay Pickard	227
Mrs. Terri Tyler	408
Mr. Dan Williams	505

8. Mr. Al Sharpe, a newly hired CPA (certified public accountant), will have his name added to the above alphabetized building directory between

A.   Mr. Randall Landover and Mr. Jay Pickard.

B.   Mr. Jay Pickard and Mrs. Terri Tyler.

C.   Mrs. Terri Tyler and Mr. Dan Williams.

D.   Mrs. Gail Keckley and Ms. Monique Givens.

Fairview Health Clinic	Suite No.
Mrs. Amanda Chadwick, LPN	105
Dr. Ray Fiorio	213
Mr. Trent Hesnor, RN	113
Dr. Colleen Lebont	201
Ms. Patricia Mason, RN	302
Dr. Enrique Petrarch	109
Mrs. Joan Quincy, LPN	212
Dr. Evelyn Spinnaker	307
Mr.Bill Thornton, LPN	311

9. Dr. Tad Ross, a new general practitioner in the Fairview Health Clinic, will have his name added to the above alphabetized directory between

A.   Dr. Colleen Lebont and Ms. Patricia Mason, LPN.

B.   Dr. Enrique Petrarch and Mrs. Joan Quincy, LPN.

C.   Dr. Evelyn Spinnaker and Mr. Bill Thornton, LPN.

D.   Mrs. Joan Quincy, LPN and Dr. Evelyn Spinnaker.

10. If the guide words *graft - grubby* were at the top of a page in the dictionary, which entry could be included on that page?

A.   gross   B.   graduation   C.   grudge   D.   graceful

THESAURUS

A thesaurus is a book containing lists of synonyms and antonyms in alphabetical order. A thesaurus improves writing and one's knowledge of words.

Thesaurus Entry

---

88. HEIGHT

NOUNS:

1. height, tip, stature, elevation
2. top, highest point, ceiling, zenith
3. hill, knoll, volcano, mountain

VERBS:

4. heighten, elevate, raise, rear, erect
5. intensify, strengthen, increase, advance
6. command, rise above, crown, surmount

ADJECTIVES:

7. high, towering, exalted, supreme

Antonyms: depth, descent

Practice 2: Thesaurus

For Questions 1 – 3, circle the word that would best provide a synonym for the italicized word in each sentence below. Then answer questions 4 – 8.

1. With a *height* of 20,320 feet, Mt. McKinley is an impressive sight.   **stature   top   elevation**

2. The *high* skyscraper stood in the center of the city.   **exalted   supreme   towering**

3. The frequent thunder *heightened* our fears for Latasha's safety.   **intensified   erected   crowned**

4. **T or F**   Increase is the same part of speech as heighten.

5. **T or F**   A mountain is lower than a hill.

6. What part of speech is **height**? _____

7. What are the antonyms for **height**? _____

8. List the synonyms for **high**. _____

ALMANACS

Almanacs are yearly publications. They appear at the beginning of each year and have articles about events of the previous year as well as expectations for the upcoming year. Almanacs are often organized by day or month of the year. Since almanacs are published every year, the information in them is current and timely.

One of the most well known almanacs is the Farmer's Almanac. The information in a farmer's almanac looks at current weather patterns, the best planting time, the kind of winter to expect, and other topics for people who are interested in nature and farming. Other almanacs focus on different areas of interest. For instance, the *Time Almanac,* from *Time Magazine,* covers various social and political topics, such as the World Series of Baseball, federal elections, holidays, and developments on the internet. *The World Almanac for Kids* features articles on current news events, movies, science, sports and other subjects of interest to young people.

An **atlas** is a book of maps and other information about countries and regions of the world. Atlases also contain information about the countries, including charts, tables and text about population, climate, resources, history, and other topics. Atlases are usually much wider and taller than most other books. This is because they contain detailed maps, which cannot fit on regular sized pages. *The Hammond Atlas of the World* is one example of a world atlas.

Books of maps are similar to atlases, and some map Web sites such as mapquest.com are helpful for traveling to various locations.

MAGAZINES

Magazines are good resources for current information. They are published weekly, semimonthly (twice per month), monthly, or quarterly (four times per year). They are also good for a variety of information because they contain articles from many different writers. Libraries classify magazines and journals as **periodicals** (published *periodically*—weekly, monthly, and so on).

Magazines usually offer articles in a specific area of interest. They are written both to inform and to entertain. Magazine articles inform readers but can also express the writer's opinion. *People* is a popular magazine that features articles about celebrities and entertainers. *Time* is a news magazine which contains articles on current events and politics. Articles in magazines like *Time* are usually detailed and well researched.

Journals are academic magazines that have information about specific areas of study. Since experts in each field write the articles, journals are considered unbiased, reliable sources of information. For example, the journal *Nature* features science articles and has the latest research in areas such as biology and geology. Journals can be found in bookstores and in libraries. *Discover* is an example of a journal which is available online for free.

Practice 3: Magazines

Gathering information from magazines. Find three articles to share with your class or instructor that could only be found in a magazine. Explain why the articles would not be found in any other resource.

SECTIONS OF A BOOK

Each textbook will include each of several sections to help the reader acquire knowledge. Listed below is each of the sections of a book found when reading from front to back.

Title Page	This page displays the title of the book, the name(s) of the author(s), edition (if the book has been published before), copyright (date the book was published), publishing company, and place of publication.
Preface	This section provides an explanatory statement about the book, telling the book's history, purpose, or plan.
Table of Contents	This section lists all the parts of the book including the introduction, the chapter titles, chapter subheadings, and page numbers indicating where each chapter begins, as well as the additional material pages.
Appendix	This part of the book contains additional material that is not essential to the text itself. This material includes charts, documents, tables, illustrations, and/or photographs. The appendix is located at the end of the text.
Glossary	This section is a dictionary of the specialized terms at the end of a book. Definitions are written in a clear and brief manner; they are also arranged in alphabetical order. The glossary contains all the terms and words that were boldfaced or italicized in the text of each chapter.
Index	This part appears at the end of the book and contains the most important topics, headings, and subheadings discussed in the textbook. The index items are arranged alphabetically with their page number reference and include important people, places, events, locations, equations, and/or books.
Bibliography	This section contains the references or citations the author(s) used while writing their book. Each reference includes the title of the work, the name(s) of the author(s), the date of publishing, publishing company, location of the publisher, and page numbers.

Practice 4: Sections of a Book

Read the following questions and select the best answer based on the information about sections of a book.

1. Which part of the book would you use to locate a table referred to in the book?

    A. bibliography   B. appendix   C. title page   D. glossary

2. The *preface* is the part of the book that gives
   A.   the explanatory statement of the book.
   B.   the citations of authors who wrote the textbook.
   C.   the publisher's name and address.
   D.   the chapter subheadings.

3. Which part of the book is used to find the sources used in writing a book?
   A.   table of contents
   B.   appendix
   C.   bibliography
   D.   title page

4. Which part of the book would you use to locate the definition of "paleontology"?
   A.   index
   B.   glossary
   C.   bibliography
   D.   preface

5. The *table of contents* is the part of the book that gives a list of
   A.   the author's name and publisher.
   B.   the title of the book.
   C.   the key words and definitions.
   D.   the section and chapter names with their starting page numbers.

6. Which part of the book is used to find the name of the publishing company for a book?
   A.   title page
   B.   index
   C.   appendix
   D.   bibliography

7. Which part of the book would you use to locate the page number for a reference on the word "self-actualization"?
   A.   index
   B.   table of contents
   C.   glossary
   D.   bibliography

8. The *appendix* is the part of a book that gives information about
   A.   chapters and page numbers.
   B.   contributing author's names.
   C.   tables, charts, and graphs referenced in the book.
   D.   the definition of a particular word found in the book.

9. Which part of the book is used to find the introduction to the book?
   A.   preface
   B.   glossary
   C.   table of contents
   D.   bibliography

10. Which part of the book is used to find the page number for the beginning of chapter 5?
   A.   appendix
   B.   glossary
   C.   preface
   D.   table of contents

TABLE OF CONTENTS

The **table of contents** is a listing of chapters and topics. A table of contents appears in the front of a book and provides an overview of the content and organization of a book.

Sample Table of Contents

Practice 5: Table of Contents

1. In which chapter would you find information on life expectancy? _____

2. On which page does the section on religion start? _____

3. If you wanted to find statistics about marriage and divorce, on which page of the book would you look? _____

4. Which chapter would you read if you wanted to find out how much money is spent on health?_____

5. In which chapter would you find facts about immigration? _____

6. What is the last page dealing with Insurance coverage? _____

INDEX

A **Book Index** is an alphabetical list of topics in a book with the page numbers referenced. The index generally contains every topic mentioned in a book and tells you which pages discuss the topic. An index appears at the end of a book.

Sample Index

Namibia, diamonds 22	New Zealand, geysers 12
Naples 13	waterfalls 44
neap tide 21	nickel 11
nectar 32, 34	Nile River 18 – 19, 43
Neptune 4	noise, loudest 42
New Guinea, area 42	nomad 37
	North Africa, deserts 37, 44

Practice 6: Index

1. On which pages are deserts discussed?_____

2. Where would you read about the loudest noise? _____

3. On which page is a major city in Italy mentioned? _____

4. What are New Zealand's two famous attractions? _____

5. Where would you find out more about the Nile River? _____

6. On which pages is nectar discussed? _____

7. In what country can you find diamonds? _____

8. On what page would you find information about nickel? _____

9. Look up six topics in another book index. List each topic and the page numbers about the topic here.

_____   _____

_____   _____

_____   _____

BIBLIOGRAPHY

A **Bibliography** is a list of writings about a particular author or topic. The writings consist of books or periodicals in alphabetical order by author's last name. A periodical is a magazine such as **National Geographic** or **Reader's Digest.** If the source is a magazine, the title of the article is in quotation marks. The name of the magazine is underlined. Titles of books are also underlined.

Practice 7: Bibliography

Read the sample bibliography following, and answer the questions that follow.

Sample Bibliography

Burnett, Frances Hodgson. The Secret Garden. New York: TDA, 1988.

Byars, Betsy. The Summer of the Swans. New York: Scholastic, 1970.

Keller, Helen. The Story of My Life. New York: Dell, 1965.

Reagan, C. & Stoner, G. "Great Stories For Children." Children Today 23 (1998): 76-77.

Sterling, Dorothy. Freedom Train. New York: Scholastic, 1954.

Verne, Jules. 20,000 Leagues Under The Sea. New York: Bantam, 1962.

Zeller, Hellen. "Games Children Play." Social Issues 11: (1997): 331-334.

---

1. Which listing in the bibliography is listed first? _____

2. Who is the author of *Story Of My Life*?_____

3. Which publishing company published the book by Jules Verne? _____

4. Which magazine has an article about children playing games?_____

5. Which book was published in 1962? _____

6. Where was *The Secret Garden* published? _____

7. How many sources listed are magazine articles? _____

8. Which book is the story of Helen Keller?_____

9. Which article has two authors? _____

10. Who is the author of *The Summer of the Swans*?_____

GLOSSARY

A **Glossary** is an alphabetical list of specialized words with their definitions. The glossary is placed at the end of a book. Glossaries are found in science, social studies, literature, math books, and many others as well.

Sample Glossary Page

monogamy - marriage to one person at a time.

monopoly - one company dominating a particular market such as cars or telephones.

monotheism - belief in one god.

mores - standards of conduct that are held by a particular culture.

multiculturalism - respecting and accepting many cultures.

national health service - health care for all citizens regardless of income.

nationalism - one nation having more rights than another nation.

net financial assets - what we own minus what we owe.

nuclear family - a group consisting of two parents and their children.

occupation - a job for pay.

Practice 8: Glossary

1. What is belief in one god called? _____

2. True or False. Volunteering to care for pre-school age children is an occupation.

3. True or False. Arriving at school on time is an example of a more.

4. True or False. A savings account is part of net financial assets.

5. Affordable medical care is called _____

6. True or False. Racism is part of muticulturalism.

7. What is being married to one person called? _____

8. True or False. Nationalism occurs when everyone in the world is treated equally.

9. True or False. A single father with two children is a nuclear family.

10. When does a company become a monopoly? _____

_____

ENCYCLOPEDIA

An **Encyclopedia** is a reference work, found in libraries or on the internet, containing articles on a variety of subjects such as people, places, historical events, science, and technology. The articles are arranged alphabetically in volumes. Specialized encyclopedias on art, music, law, technology, and literature are also available in libraries and on the internet.

Sample Encyclopedia Page

CAVY, *KAYvee,* is the common name for several related South American *rodents* (gnawing animals). Common cavies are called *guinea pigs.* Other cavies include *maras (Patagonian hares) and mocos.* Most cavies have fat bodies, short legs, and stiff, bristly hair. Maras have long, thin legs. A few kinds of *domesticated* (tamed) guinea pigs have long hair. All cavies eat plants or seeds.

CAYENNE PEPPER, a hot spice made from a plant called capiscum frutescens.

CAYMAN ISLANDS, A British dependency, located about 200 miles (320 kilometers) northwest of Jamaica in the Caribbean Sea. The three islands that make up the Cayman Islands are named Grand Cayman, Little Cayman, and Cayman Brac. They range over 100 square miles (259 square kilometers), and have 14,000 persons. The capital and largest city, Georgetown, is on Grand Cayman, the largest island.

CAYUGA INDIANS. See Iroquois Indians.

CAYUGA LAKE. See Finger Lakes.

CBR WARFARE. See Chemical-Biological-Radiological Warfare.

Practice 9: Encyclopedia

1. In what volume would you find more information on Cayuga Lake?_____

2. What is the common name for guinea pig? _____

3. What is another name for the Iroquois Indians? _____

4. Where are the Cayman Islands? _____

5. How many islands make up the Cayman Islands? _____

6. What kind of food do maras eat? _____

7. What does CBR stand for?_____

8. What is capiscum frutescens?_____

COMPUTER RESEARCH

THE INTERNET

So much information is available on the **internet** today that it has changed the way we do research. If you are finishing a research paper and you have not yet gone "online," you have not exhausted the tools available to you. The ability to best find and use Web sites is a vital skill in this rapidly growing world of internet access. Whether you are looking for the best price for your spring break travel, finding out the details of a job you are applying for, or writing a paper for class, the internet is a valuable resource if used wisely and efficiently.

Using the internet can challenge your research skills. First, you must decide which **key words** to use and to find the material you want, instead of a lot of marketing sites or opinion based information. In addition, you must access various **search engines** such as Google, Yahoo, or Lycos to find the best Web sites about your topic. Then, you must **validate** the material, checking the site for its credibility or the material for accuracy. Next, you must decide how best to use the material and if it is an **appropriate** source for your topic. Finally, you need the skill of **safe research** on the World Wide Web.

RESEARCH KEY WORDS

Key words are tools for searching to find the most useful sites in the shortest amount of time. These key words are arranged with other words to broaden a search that is too narrow or narrowing one that is too broad.

Using as an example the art of scrimshaw, we can decide that key words include *scrimshaw*, *carving*, and *ivory*. While *scrimshaw* is specific enough that a search would probably yield good results, using just the word *carving* would be too broad. In that case you might combine it, for example with *ivory*, to narrow your search and access more relevant material.

1. Make a list of words that describe what you are looking for in a site, such as words that you would use in describing the topic to a friend. Use those words for a first search.

2. Next, make a list of synonyms for these words. This will give you ways to narrow your topic.

3. Try using both the singular and plural forms of the search words for your topic.

4. Be careful how you use abbreviations and numerals, such as in WWII. Also, check the spelling, hyphens, and spacing of your key words before you click on the search button.

5. For certain databases, use methods of searching like the Boolean Method, using the words "**AND, OR, NOT**" to either expand or restrict your search. You may also use quotation marks or the plus sign to refine a search.

VALIDATION: CHECKING SOURCES

Why should you bother with validating sources? After all, if you can find material on a Web site, it must be OK, right? No, not always. Many Web sites are created by students and ordinary citizens, who may believe what they have posted is true, but are mistaken in that belief: "Let the searcher beware!" Researchers protect their work by screening the material they find for quality and accuracy.

1. Find two or more sources that agree with the information you wish to use.

2. Read the material carefully, watching for bias or particularly strong opinion.

3. Look at the **URL (Uniform Resource Locator**, otherwise known as the Web address) for the source of the material, which is usually an organization or individual. If the organization is an educational, government, or professional center, the material is probably valid.

4. Look for "links" within the text of a Web site; these are an indication of a serious, validated work (they're like footnotes in a book). Go to some of the linked sites to check the validity of the sources, as well as to find additional material.

5. Look at the homepage of the source for other related works by the author of the site. The more the author has published on a topic, the more trustworthy the material.

6. Check the date on the material. Obviously if your topic is on a current event, the more recent the date, the better the information. Also keep in mind that recent data and theories are valuable for any topic.

7. If you are using informal sources, such as chat rooms, for clustering or sharing ideas, again, the information needs to be confirmed by two or more other sources before it is validated.

Some sites on the internet have been validated already. These are listed in **database sites**. The organization which creates the database checks the material to ensure both accuracy and relevancy. Many databases are offered through educational organizations and are free to all. One example is *thinkquest.com,* a site that indexes award-winning, student-created Web sites. The site covers many topics and many levels of study. One word of caution: **Plagiarism** or copying directly from a source is a serious offense; be sure to always cite your Internet sources. If you want to use a reproduction of material, as on this page, get written permission from the Web site owner to use it.

Now, look at the three examples of Web pages that follow, each showing a different structure and focus for a Web search of "fossils." Notice the focus of the pages, and decide which would be the most appropriate source of information in a Web search for fossils.

Web Site I—Notice the name of the organization that established this Web site. If you scan the page, you see that this is an advertisement. While it is attractive and well-formatted, there is no educational material here. Validation for this example is simple; it is not an appropriate or relevant source for scholarly research.

Web Site II—The next Web site is an example of a site that has relevant information but lacks the background of serious educational focus. It is well-written and attractive in structure. The facts may be accurate but should be double-checked against other sources before being used.

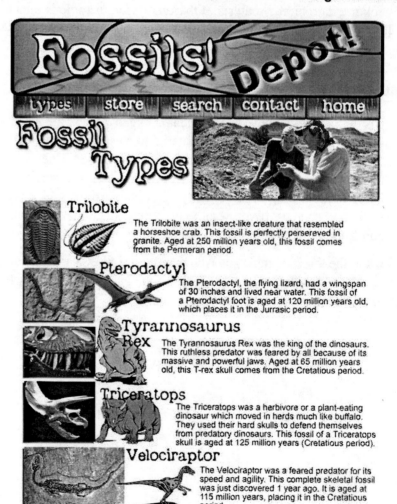

Web Site III—This example is of a printed Web page. The information that is needed to validate the material is labeled.

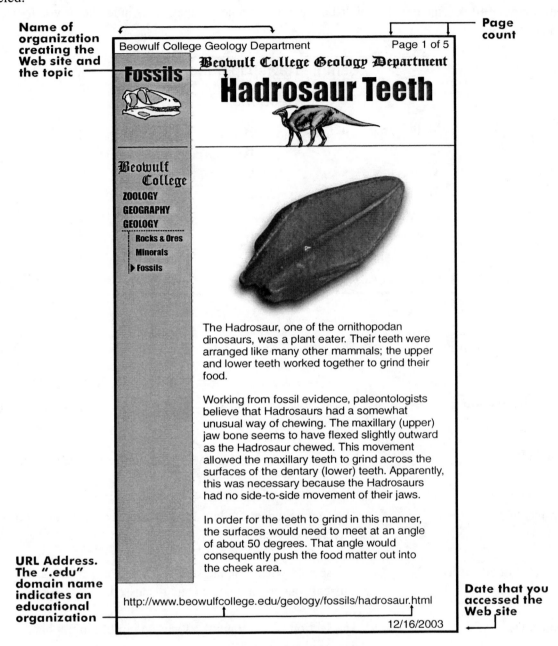

Name of organization creating the Web site and the topic

Page count

Beowulf College Geology Department   Page 1 of 5

Beowulf College Geology Department

Hadrosaur Teeth

Fossils

Beowulf College
ZOOLOGY
GEOGRAPHY
GEOLOGY
   Rocks & Ores
   Minerals
   Fossils

The Hadrosaur, one of the ornithopodan dinosaurs, was a plant eater. Their teeth were arranged like many other mammals; the upper and lower teeth worked together to grind their food.

Working from fossil evidence, paleontologists believe that Hadrosaurs had a somewhat unusual way of chewing. The maxillary (upper) jaw bone seems to have flexed slightly outward as the Hadrosaur chewed. This movement allowed the maxillary teeth to grind across the surfaces of the dentary (lower) teeth. Apparently, this was necessary because the Hadrosaurs had no side-to-side movement of their jaws.

In order for the teeth to grind in this manner, the surfaces would need to meet at an angle of about 50 degrees. That angle would consequently push the food matter out into the cheek area.

URL Address. The ".edu" domain name indicates an educational organization

http://www.beowulfcollege.edu/geology/fossils/hadrosaur.html

12/16/2003

Date that you accessed the Web site

Practice 10: Using Web Sites

Choose a topic to research on the internet. Use a subject that could possibly be a school assignment. Search for your topic on the internet, and then, look at several of the Web sites. Identify the following types of sites, and print out one page from each. Find one site that is an unreliable source, one that is questionable, and one that is definitely a reliable source. On the back of each printed page, explain why you believe each site is reliable, unreliable, or questionable. Indicate what information you used to make your judgements.

NEWSPAPER INDEX AND NEWSPAPER AD

A **Newspaper Index** is an alphabetical list of sections in a newspaper. This index helps you locate articles on a particular topic.

Sample Newspaper Index	
Sections	
Main News/Front Page	A
Editorials	B
Travel	C
Sports	D
Entertainment	E
Obituaries	F
Advertisements	G
Classified Ads	H

Main News/Front Page	The page and section where the most important news items are printed.
Editorial Section	The section where the editors' or publisher's opinions on some subjects are printed.
Travel Section	The section where information about different areas of the world and prices of travel are printed.
Sports Section	The section where the latest sports events and famous sports players are discussed.
Entertainment Section	The section where the latest movies, theater performances, and musical concerts are posted and discussed.
Obituaries	The section where funeral notices and brief biographies of the deceased are posted.
Advertisements	Public notices or announcements recommending certain products or services.
Classified Section	The section where notices of employment opportunities, homes for sale, apartments for rent, lost and found, etc. are posted.

Practice 11: Newspaper

Tell in which section you would look for the following articles.

1. Where would you find an article about a major earthquake in China?_____

2. Where would you find news about the state basketball playoffs?_____

3. What would you find in the obituaries?_____

4. Where would the movie listings appear?_____

5. Where would you find the time and place of a movie you want to see?_____

6. Where would you look for the cheapest plane fare to New York? _____

7. Where would you look to find the details on the time for a funeral? _____

8. Where would you find the editors' opinions on the latest government crisis?_____

9. Where would you find the department store sales this week? _____

10. What would you find in the classified section? _____

11. What would you expect to find on the front page?_____

A **Newspaper (Classified) Ad** is a notice designed to promote a product, service, or business. Newspaper ads vary in size, shape, and color and are often created to increase sales or to offer employment.

> Fine dining restaurant in Liberty now hiring hostess, cooks, servers, and bussers. Will work around your school schedule. Jobs pay between $5 – $8 per hour. Ask for Sandra or Keva. Apply at 461 Whistle St. or phone 889-4200.

Practice 12: Newspaper Ad

1. What is the address of the restaurant? _____

2. When are the workers needed? _____

3. Whom should you speak with about the positions? _____

4. Since the employer works around a school schedule, who is the main audience for the ad?

_____

QUESTIONS ABOUT REFERENCE SOURCES

Tips for Questions About Reference Sources
1. Skim through the reference source.
2. Read the reference source two or three times. Become familiar with the format and organization of the reference.
3. Read the question carefully.
4. Scan the reference source to find your answer.
5. Confirm your answer by reviewing the evidence in the source.

CHOOSING THE RIGHT REFERENCE SOURCES

In the first part of this chapter, you learned about important **resource materials**. Then, you practiced answering questions about them. Now is a good time to learn to choose the best resource material for your needs.

Let's say that you are doing a report on cowhands. Several sources may give some information about cowhands, but only a few sources will give you enough material for a report. For example, a **dictionary** will give you a definition of cowhand. A **bibliography** might list some books about cowhands. The **electronic card catalog** can help you locate the books about cowhands if you have any in your library. You might even locate a **map** of states where cowhands live. However, only one or two reference sources will provide enough information for a report. Most likely this information will come from longer articles in an **encyclopedia** (in book form or in **computer software**), or from educational sites on the **internet**.

Based on the above example, you can see that choosing the right reference source means:

- Clearly defining your own research needs,
- Being familiar with different resources and their strengths, and
- Being able to use each form of resource material easily.

In the chapter review, you'll be identifying the best resource for obtaining information on a particular topic or problem. Before you start answering the questions, review the main resource materials from this chapter.

CHAPTER 9 REVIEW

Read each question. Then choose the appropriate source for finding the information.

1. Sonya wants to write to Danny Haren of the St. Louis Cardinals. Where would she look?

    A. dictionary   B. thesaurus   C. internet   D. almanac

2. Josh found a gold watch in the woods with no identification. Where would he find the owner?

    A. newspaper ad   B. encyclopedia   C. internet   D. thesaurus

3. Diane is writing a paper and needs another word to use for the word "trip." Which reference should she use?

    A. appendix   B. bibliography   C. thesaurus   D. encyclopedia

4. Shawn is buying his first car. Where would he look for the best price?

    A. computer software   C. table of contents

    B. newspaper ads   D. bibliography

5. Aaron wants to find out which page in his history book tells about the causes of World War I. What part of the book should he look in?

    A. bibliography   B. appendix   C. index   D. title page

6. Zack needs to know the page number for the beginning of Chapter 6. Where should he look?

    A. index   B. table of con-   C. bibliography   D. appendix
                               tents

7. Brittany needs to know the definition of the word "lugubrious." Where should she look?

    A. dictionary   B. thesaurus   C. internet   D. encyclopedia

8. Charles needs to do a report on sea creatures that dwell on the bottom of the ocean. Which of the following resources would he most likely **not** turn to?

    A. encyclopedia   B. internet   C. newspaper   D. library
                                                          index

Marketing and Sales Division Building	
	Office No.
Mr. Arnold Bass	218
Ms Susan Chapel	128
Mr. Dale Fletcher	222
Mr. Ken Greene	207
Mrs. Cheryl Love	105
Ms Gail Spears	109
Mr. Ben Tinley	215
Mrs. Jessie Ulrich	112
Mr. Sam Walton	111

9. Ms. Stone, a new accounts manager in the Marketing and Sales Division Building, will have her name added to the alphabetized building directory on the preceding page between

   A. Mrs. Cheryl Love and Ms. Gail Spears.

   B. Mr. Ben Tinley and Mrs. Jessie Ulrich.

   C. Ms. Gail Spears and Mr. Ben Tinley.

   D. Ms. Susan Chapel and Mr. Dale Fletcher.

10. If the guide words *lance - late* were at the top of a page in the dictionary, which word could be included on that page?

   A. laundry   B. laser   C. lamp   D. lake

11. Where would you find alphabetized definitions of terms describing the body in a biology book?

   A. table of contents   C. bibliography

   B. index   D. glossary

```
Statistical Index

Space Research and Technology,
Federal Outlays.........................509, 983
Spain. See Foreign Countries
Spanish-American War, cost................548
Spices, imports.....................1105,1107,1109
Sporting and athletic goods
Sports............................407,408,1130
Consumer Price Indexes..........................748
Sporting goods and bicycle shops,
retail................................1278
Sports............................309,404,412
Expenditures...................................393,407
Sports Associations....................................92
Sports Industry Receipts..........................395
Spot Market Price Index..........................760
Squid..............................................1152,1158
```

12. On what page(s) would you find information about pepper and cloves?

   A. 1109

   B. 760

   C. 983

   D. 393

CHAPTER 9 TEST

Read each question then choose the appropriate source for finding the information.

1. Which source would you use for buying a portable compact disc player?

   A. newspaper   B. encyclopedia   C. glossary   D. book index

2. If Kelsey were lost in the mall, where would she look for help?

   A. index   B. dictionary   C. map   D. internet

3. Where would you search to find the origin of the word **numeral?**
   A. dictionary   B. encyclopedia   C. glossary   D. book index

4. Orlando wants to watch the Super Bowl on television tomorrow, but he can't remember when it starts. Where should he look?
   A. newspaper   B. encyclopedia   C. internet   D. magazine

5. Teresa is doing research on the Ebola virus for a class project. Which is the best source for her to use to get started?
   A. thesaurus   B. dictionary   C. internet   D. glossary

6. The senior class trip will be a long bus drive from Miami to New York. What is the best source for travel plans?
   A. atlas   B. encyclopedia   C. directory   D. bibliography

7. Don wants to find out what the weather will be like at the beach this weekend. What source would be the most helpful?
   A. glossary   B. newspaper   C. thesaurus   D. encyclopedia

8. The International Food Festival is next week, and everyone must bring food from another country. Where will Fatima find a dish to make?
   A. index   B. encyclopedia   C. glossary   D. recipe book

9. Where would you look for a list of the players on this year's All-American high school basketball team?
   A. magazine   B. internet   C. newspaper ad   D. glossary

10. Where would you look for a picture of the current Miss America?
    A. encyclopedia   B. internet   C. atlas   D. glossary

11. Sondra wants to write to the publishing company of a book that she has. Where should she look for the address?
    A. index   B. glossary   C. table of contents   D. title page

Participating Dentists

Lisa Andu, DDS
Stephen Campbell, DDS
John Glasser, DDS
Peggy King, DDS
Paul McLendon, DDS
D. Janet Taylor, DDS
Gary Terkiewicz, DDS
Leigh Thomaston, DDS
Marysia Triggs, DDS
Brenda Warner, DDS

12. Harry K. Telzig will be added to the alphabetized list of participating dentists in the dental plan. His name will be added between
    A. Leigh Thomaston, DDS and Marysia Triggs, DDS.
    B. D. Janet Taylor, DDS and Gary Terkiewicz, DDS.
    C. Gary Terkiewicz and Leigh Thomaston, DDS.
    D. Marysia Triggs, DDS and Brenda Warner, DDS.

13. In the entertainment section of the newspaper, you would find information about
    A. where to purchase concert tickets.   C. plane crashes.
    B. a missing dog.   D. the editor's opinions

14. In what section of the newspaper would you find opposing views on a current event?
    A. front page   C. advertisements
    B. classified section   D. editorial section

15. In the obituaries of a newspaper, you would find
    A. restaurant reviews.
    B. biographies on the recently deceased.
    C. news on medical advancements.
    D. information about basketball championships.

16. In what section of the newspaper would you find the latest department store sale?
    A. clasified section   C. obituaries
    B. advertisements   D. front page

17. Which part of a book would you use to locate additional charts and graphs not found in the book's chapters?
    A. appendix   C. table of contents
    B. glossary   D. bibliography

18. The *title page* is the part of the book that gives information on
    A. page references for the names, places, and subjects in a book.
    B. the author, title, and publication of the book.
    C. books, articles, etc., used or referred to by an author.
    D. supplementary material not essential to the text itself.

19. Which part of a book would you use to locate the page numbers that discuss the Cuban Missile Crisis?
    A. title page   B. index   C. glossary   D. appendix

20. Which part of a book would you use to find other writings on a specific subject referred to by the author?
    A. preface   B. appendix   C. glossary   D. bibliography

21. If you have the encyclopedia volume labeled <u>So-Sz</u>, which subject could you find in that volume?
    A. race relations   B. temperature   C. snow   D. spelling

Georgia 8th Grade English/Language Arts Practice Test 1

Note: All standards referenced are English Language Arts.

1. **What is the structure of the sentence below?**   8C1b

   > Kyle worked at a restaurant, he wanted to pay for his truck.

   A. compound   C. compound-complex

   B. complex   D. simple

2. **Which of the following sentences contains a misplaced modifier?**   8C1c

   A. Sara ate French fries at a restaurant full of animal fat.

   B. Last night I heard about the tsunami on the news.

   C. Our high school reported an increase in student enrollment for the third year in a row.

   D. More students reported problems opening their locker this year then ever before.

3. **How should the punctuation be corrected in the sentence below?**   8C1g

   > Everyone, including me was surprised at how much money we raised.

   A. Remove the comma after *everyone*.   C. Add a comma after *much*.

   B. Add a comma after *surprised*.   D. Add a comma after *me*.

4. **Which sentence below is a compound sentence?**   8C1b

   A. The Beatles and the Monkees sang and recorded songs over twenty years ago.

   B. I have never played baseball, but I like to watch baseball games.

   C. Because baldness is inherited, I am afraid of going bald when I get older.

   D. It was a shock to everyone when I won the contest.

5. **Which word BEST fits in the blank in the sentence below?** 8C1d

> _____ going to take your place if you leave?

A. Who	C. Who's
B. Whose	D. Whoever

6. **How would the sentence below change if** *student* **were changed to** *students?*

> The student walks to his house every day.

A. The students walk to his houses every day. 8C1d

B. The students walk to their houses every day.

C. The students walks to their house every day.

D. The student walks to their houses every day.

7. **She made two cups of hot chocolate and joined him on the <u>sofa, for</u> several minutes they just looked out at the mountains in silence.** 8C1e

A. sofa: for	C. sofa and for
B. sofa; for	D. leave as is

8. **In which of the following sentences is the case of the pronouns correct?** 8C1a

A. He and I got on the elevator at the same time.

B. We saw she and him leave the building.

C. I asked Mark and he for a ride home.

D. Us and them will be renting a movie tonight.

9. **Which of the following is a complete sentence?** 8C1b

A. She sat quickly

B. She nodded she sipped coffee.

C. The dog ran I followed.

D. A person who is loyal.

10. **Which of the following is a fragment?**

A. She ran the race. 8C1b

B. Working after school.

C. Sheila went upstairs.

D. I have measles.

11. **Which sentence below is written correctly?** 8C1g

A. Mom looked at her daughter and asked? "do you like your new jeans"?

B. Mom looked at her daughter and asked, "Do you like your new jeans"?

C. Mom looked at her daughter and asked, "do you like your new jeans?"

D. Mom looked at her daughter and asked, "Do you like your new jeans?"

12. **Which would be a good topic sentence to begin the second paragraph of the passage below?** 8W1

One of the highest compliments you can give a man is to call him a "Renaissance man." It means he is brilliant and can do many kind of work extremely well. People use this phrase to describe the famous artist from the Renaissance, Leonardo da Vinci.

A. Leonardo was born in 1452 in the small Italian town of Vinci.

B. Later he became famous because he was able to do sculpture as well as he painted.

C. Leonardo, also a great inventor, experimented with everything including the paints he used.

D. The paint Leonardo used absorbed moisture from the wall and his famous painting, *The Last Supper*, began to crumble and its bright colors became dull.

13. In the sentence below, which pronouns belong in the spaces? 8C1a

> After dinner, _____ and _____ went for a walk.

A. he; her

B. he; her

C. she; I

D. she; him

14. Which words make up the adjective clause in the following sentence? 8C1f

> I am often tired after I go to school all week.

A. am often tired.

B. often tired

C. to school all week

D. after I go to school all week

Use the outline below to answer the question which follows.

> I   Pyramids of Egypt
>   A. What is a pyramid?
>   1. mummies
>   2. hieroglyphics
>   B. When they were built?
>   1. Old kingdom pyramids
>   2. The Great pyramid
>   C. How pyramids were built
>   1. materials
>   2. labor
>
> II.   Pyramids of South America
>   A. What is a pyramid?
>   1. mummies
>   2. hieroglyphics
>   B. When they were built?
>   1. Oldest (in Peru)
>   2. The Great pyramid
>   C. How pyramids were built
>   1. materials
>   2. labor

15. Where would the additional entry _"Hidden inside chambers"_ fit in the outline above? 8W1

A. I. C. 3

B. I. B. 3

C. I. A. 3

D. I. D. 1

16. Which word makes a transition in the paragraph below? 8W1

> _President Teddy Roosevelt loved the outdoors. When he was president, he signed laws to prevent too much logging and mining in the country wilderness. He began a conservation effort protecting our national forests. As a result the number of national parks doubled under his administration. Consequently, many of the national parks we have today were created through the efforts of President Theodore Roosevelt._

A. Consequently

B. result

C. began

D. doubled

17. Read the sentence below. Then identify the underlined part of the sentence. 8C1f

> _I came because I was invited._

A. adverb clause

B. prepositional phrase

C. independent clause

D. adjective clause

18. Choose the sentence in which the apostrophe is used correctly. 8C1g

A. I like the deck on the Sanders' house.

B. The lights' of Mobile can be seen across the causeway.

C. The childrens' shoes were caked with mud.

D. A firemans' gear is very heavy.

19. Read the paragraph. Choose the line in which an apostrophe is needed. 8C1g

(1)Rod asked the farrier to shoe his horses. (2)The farrier said that the horses hooves were split. (3)He trimmed their hooves. (4)Then he shod both horses.

A. 1   B. 2   C. 3   D. 4

20. Read the paragraph. Choose the sentence that BEST fits the blank in the paragraph. 8W1

_____. _Their mother told them that she would take them if they cleaned the bedroom that they shared. The children hurried to their room and began picking up scattered toys. When they had picked up their toys, they smiled and told their mother that they were ready to go to the park._

A. A mother and her two children were watching television.

B. Two children asked their mother to take them to the park.

C. Two children skipped into the kitchen where their mother was preparing lunch.

D. A mother and her two children cleared the table and cleaned the kitchen after lunch.

21. Read the paragraph. Choose the sentence that BEST fills in the blank in the paragraph. 8W1

_Mrs. Jernigan taught school for twenty-five years. _____. She often said, "If you don't have time to do it right, when will you have time to do it again?" Even though I have not seen Mrs. Jernigan in over ten years, her words continue to influence me._

A. She was my eleventh grade English teacher.

B. She taught in the school that she had attended as a student.

C. She used a variety of instructional methods.

D. She always encouraged her students to do their best.

22. Read the paragraph. Choose the sentence that does NOT belong in the paragraph.

Josephine Mallard was told that her husband had died in a train accident. (2) Josephine was a well-to-do woman, afflicted with heart trouble.(3) Several hours later Bentley Mallard returned home, composed and carrying his attaché case. (4) He had been far away from the scene of the accident and did not know there had even been one. 8W1

A. Sentence 1   C. Sentence 3

B. Sentence 2   D. Sentence 4

23. Read the paragraph. Choose the sentence that does NOT belong in the paragraph.

(1) Bill and Maxine have been married for over fifty years. (2) They enjoy traveling and seeing new places. (3) Maxine is an excellent cook and prepares delicious meals. (4) They plan to tour Europe next summer. 8W1

A. Sentence 1   C. Sentence 3

B. Sentence 2   D. Sentence 4

24. Read the paragraph. Choose the sentence that would be the BEST concluding sentence. 8W1

> Schools are trying to help keep students fit. Many schools are banning sugary soda in elementary and middle schools. Only water and fruit juices will be sold.

A. Soft drinks should be taken only in moderation.

B. Juice and water are very good for you.

C. Exercise also helps keep students fit.

D. This is expected to begin in the next month.

25. Read the sentence. Choose the transitional word or words that BEST fit the blank. 8W1.

> The heavy rainfall kept the children inside; _____, they had a good time building a fort in the den

A. besides

B. otherwise

C. that is

D. nevertheless

26. Read the four sentences. Then choose the answer that shows the BEST order for the sentences. 8W1

1. First they went to Movie Village and chose three movies.

2. Then they went home and popped popcorn.

3. Marissa and Sierra decided to rent movies.

4. They put a movie in the VCR and settled back for a pleasant night.

A. 3, 1, 2, 4

B. 2, 3, 1, 4

C. 2, 1, 3, 4

D. 4, 1, 2, 3

27. Choose the sentence in which the apostrophe is used correctly. 8C1g

A. We sometimes value other peoples' opinions more than our own.

B. Cheyenne bought tickets to a Harlem Globetrotter's game.

C. The jury listened to the clerk's testimonies.

D. Dusty's taking Diana to the prom.

28. Choose the sentence that contains an error in punctuation. 8C1e

A. No, I do not understand the question.

B. Have you seen my dress Mom?

C. On March 16, 1978, Misty Lynn was born.

D. The reunion will be held September 2010.

29. Which words make up the adjective clause in the following sentence? 8C1f

> Mary Smith, who is my favorite aunt, is coming over today to bring my birthday present.

A. is coming over today

B. birthday present

C. who is my favorite aunt

D. to bring my birthday present

30. Identify the total number of underlined words that have capitalization errors. 8C1g

> The student asked, "how many times did columbus travel to the New world?"

A. one

B. two

C. three

D. four

Select the sentence in each group that is *incorrectly* punctuated.

31. A. Every person in this nation has the following rights: life, liberty, and the pursuit of happiness. 8C1g

B. Dear Senator Helms:

C. At 245 p.m., my flight is scheduled to begin boarding.

D. My favorite foods are as follows: pizza, lasagna, and roast beef.

32. A. If you want to win, "the coach said," you have to pay the price of winning.

B. "Attention! Forward march!" yelled the drill sergeant. 8C1g

C. Martha Dwire says that these people are very intelligent.

D. The sign in the restaurant read, "No smoking, please."

33. A. Their activities included the following: playing capture the flag, telling ghost stories, and building a campfire. 8C1e

B. The train arrived promptly at 7:30 p.m.

C. These responsibilities fell on Geor-gette: washing the car, feeding the dog, and watering the plants

D. To Whom it May Concern,

34. A. The lions at the zoo were fed a diet of fresh beef and rodents. 8C1g

B. The biology students were given three minutes to examine each organism.

C. The new virus was sent to the Center for Disease Control in Atlanta Georgia.

D. Zena threw her spear at the lizard man and skewered him.

35. A. The center of the highway was eaten by a large, scaly creature. 8C1e

B. The happy-go-lucky cat was chased by the snarling dog.

C. Kramer's apartment caught on fire, when he tried to iron his shirt.

D. Jerry's car was repainted orange by his friend, Sal.

For questions 36 & 37, identify the sentence in which the underlined pronoun is used correctly.

36. A. Shirley runs the race faster than <u>them</u>.

B. <u>Who</u> is the package for? 8C1a

C. He wants to join with <u>us</u> this year.

D. <u>Him</u> have a new computer system at home.

37. A. I vote for the candidate <u>me</u> trust most.

B. We will soar close to the mountains when it's <u>our</u> turn. 8C1a

C. Currently, <u>him</u> builds new apartments with me.

D. Karen and <u>her</u> cooked the goose.

38. **What is the structure of the sentence below?** 8C1b

> The guitar has only 4 strings, but it is difficult to play.

A. Simple

B. Compound

C. Complex

D. Compound-complex

39. **Read the paragraph. Choose the sentence that would be the BEST concluding sentence.** 8W1

> The most common type of nonfatal injury in teenagers is sports injuries. Approximately one out of fourteen teenagers has required hospitalization for a sports injury. Football caused nearly 20 percent of these injuries.

A. Car accidents, drownings, and sports injuries occur frequently among teenagers.

B. Baseball is one of the safest sports to play.

C. Sports are fun and keep teenagers fit and healthy.

D. Basketball, baseball, and skating caused most of the other injuries.

40. **Read the sentence. Choose the word or words that BEST fit the blank.** 8W1

> I am going to borrow my dad's car;_____,I have to wash it first.

A. besides   C. that is

B. otherwise   D. however

41. Read the four sentences. Then choose the answer that shows the BEST order for the sentences. 8W1

1. First they asked their parents' permission.

2. Then they checked the "help wanted" board at school.

3. Shona and Cheri decided to work after school.

4. They both went to work at a neighborhood video store.

A. 3, 1, 2, 4   C. 2, 1, 3, 4

B. 2, 3, 1, 4   D. 4, 1, 2, 3

42. Which sentence below contains an error?

A. This kind of skating requires practice.

B. Jill, not John and Vance, has drawn that picture. 8C1g

C. My cat, as well as my two dogs, needs fresh water every day.

D. Did Cameron say he was coming to the party.

43. Choose the sentence that is punctuated correctly. 8C1g

A. Mason, said Libby, "I need to go to the library after school."

B. "Mason," said Libby, "I need to go to the library after school."

C. "Mason, said Libby," I need to go to the library after school.

D. "Mason," said Libby, "I need to go to the library after school.

44. Identify the sentence with incorrect punctuation. 8C1e

A. Monica applied for ten scholarships; consequently, she was not surprised when she was offered one.

B. The following students won the writing contest: Linda Sinclair, senior; Mindi Goolsby, junior; and Aaron Raines, sophomore.

C. My favorite hobbies are: collecting coins, building model airplanes, and gardening.

D. Jeannie likes sewing; she also enjoys baking.

45. Choose the answer that is a fragment.

A. Kirsten sang. 8C1b

B. When the two campers set up their tent.

C. The bikers rode for thirty-three miles.

D. I finished the book.

46. Choose the answer that is a complete sentence. 8C1b

A. They looked both ways.

B. Before crossing the street.

C. When Stephanie and Bailey ate dessert.

D. After they had eaten a salad, a roll, and spaghetti.

47. Choose the sentence that is written correctly. 8C1a

A. My parents and they are friends.

B. Are Jarrod and him brothers?

C. The principal talked to Kalesha and myself.

D. My cousin and them are neighbors.

48. Which of the following sentences is unrelated to the main idea? 8W1

1. For six months, the Winter's planned their vacation. **2.** They ordered travel brochures. **3.** After reading brochures, they decided to go to the Grand Canyon. **4.** Last year they went to Alaska.

A. Sentence 1   C. Sentence 3

B. Sentence 2   D. Sentence 4

49. Read the following paragraph from a formal report. Choose the sentence in which the language is inappropriate. 8W2

1. The alligator is known for its strong jaws and powerful tail. **2.** Nevertheless, if you are able to put your hands around the closed jaws of an alligator, you can easily hold its jaws closed. **3.** An alligator's powerful tail makes it a strong swimmer, while its stocky legs enable it to walk on land. **4.** Although an alligator can run very fast on land, a person might outrun an alligator by running in a zigzag pattern because an alligator cannot change directions quickly.

A. Sentence 1   C. Sentence 3

B. Sentence 2   D. Sentence 4

50. What would be a good topic sentence for the second paragraph of the passage below? 8W1

What do you feed baby bunnies that have barely opened their eyes? We sure didn't know and there weren't any handy guides on the subject! I knew rabbits raided our garden every summer, so I suggested lettuce. My mom, who is a nurse, took the logical approach. "Since they're so small, they are still suckling," she said. "All they eat right now is milk." Now we were getting somewhere: we would give them milk. I was glad we had that settled because their hungry little squeals were really breaking my heart.

A. They couldn't drink from a bowl yet.

B. At first, we tried soaking the corner of a washcloth in milk and offered it to the little bunnies.

C. How do you get milk into a mouth the size of an apple seed?

D. Then my mom had an idea — she rummaged through the first aid kit until she found an eyedropper.

For questions 51 – 54, copy the following sentences, adding all missing punctuation and correcting any capitalization errors.

51. Mrs Chapman continues to write all the students grades in a notebook, she refuses to learn how to put them in a computer. 8C1e, 8C1g

52. The changing names and borders of eastern European countries makes mapmaking very difficult. 8C1d, 8C1g

53. Looking well-dressed brad and his friend bethany served the dinner friday night. 8C1c, 8C1g

54. The contestant answered it was king henry viii who started the Anglican church. 8C1e, 8C1g

For questions 55 – 56, combine the sentences into one sentence. Be sure to punctuate and capitalize correctly.

55. Jeff bought his metal bat out of the dugout. Jeff exchanged his metal bat for a wooden bat. Jeff noticed the lightning was starting to flash. 8C1b, 8C1g

56. Dan delivered the pizza to the correct house. The pizza was hot and fresh. Dan delivered the pizza with three minutes to spare. 8C1b

For questions 57 – 60, copy the sentences correcting dangling modifiers, unclear pronoun references, and adverb, adjective, or verb errors.

57. Riding the raft down the Chattahoochee River, the trees hung over the water. 8C1c, 8C1d

58. We ate the cookies quick while they were still warm. 8C1f

59. After putting the tie with the shirt, Sherri sold it. 8C1a

60. Sarah was trying to figure out who will follow her from the store yesterday. 8C1d

For questions 61 – 65, answer the question or follow the directions and write on your own paper.

61. Where would you look if you were trying to find a particular key term within a book? 8W2

62. Write two to three appropriate transition words in order by importance. 8W1

R ewrite the sentences so they are consistent with the third person point of view

63. Reynaldo looked outside his window and counted the stars until his eyelids weighed him down like barbells. "Finally, you can get some sleep," I mumbled to myself as I rolled over and turned out the lights. 8W4

64. If someone wishes to write a narrative in which he or she as the writer knows the thoughts of the characters, this person is writing from the _____point of view. 8W1

65. Dante is interested in trying out for a part in a play at Maple Woods Middle School and has been asked to write down what makes him qualified to be an actor. Which of the following three details is inappropriate and why? 8W2

    A. I know how to memorize lines quickly.

    B. I have previously acted in a community drama.

    C. I know how to write well on paper.

Georgia 8th Grade English/Language Arts Practice Test 2

Note: All standards referenced are English Language Arts

1. **What is the structure of the sentence below?**   8C1b

   > Tara got a new cell phone for her birthday, but she didn't know how to use it.

   A. compound

   B. complex

   C. compound-complex

   D. simple

2. **Which of the following sentences contains a misplaced modifier?**   8C1c

   A. Jill ordered chocolate pie at a restaurant which was topped with whipped cream.

   B. Last night I heard about a terrible tornado on the news.

   C. Our high school reported an increase in students playing sports for the third year in a row.

   D. More parents reported problems with the busses running late this year than ever before.

3. **How should the punctuation be corrected in the sentence below?**   8C1e

   > Everybody, especially Ann was surprised at how many tickets we sold.

   A. Remove the comma after *everybody*.

   B. Change were to *we're*.

   C. Add a comma after *many*.

   D. Add a comma after *Ann*.

4. **Which sentence below is a compound sentence?**   8C1b

   A. My mom and dad went to rallies and protested over twenty years ago.

   B. I have never been to Mexico, but I like to eat tacos.

   C. Because my parents are short, I am afraid I won't be able to play basketball.

   D. I played my best and I won the tournament.

5. Which word BEST fits in the blank in the sentence below? 8C1d.

> _____ going to take the dog to the vet.

A. There

C. They're

B. Their

D. Them is

6. How would the sentence below change if *dog* were changed to *dogs*? 8C1d

> The dog sleeps in the doghouse outside in the yard.

A. The dogs sleep in the dogshouse outside in the yard.

B. The dogs sleeps in the doghouse outside in the yard.

C. The dogs sleep in the doghouse outside in the yard.

D. The dogs sleeps in the dogshouse outside in the yard.

7. Which of the following sentences is punctuated correctly? 8C1e

A. "When you were so close to finishing," Jessica asked, "why did you just quit"?

B. "When you were so close to finishing, Jessica asked, why did you just quit ?"

C. "When you were so close to finishing", Jessica asked, "why did you just quit"?

D. "When you were so close to finishing," Jessica asked, "why did you just quit?"

8. In which of the following sentences is the case of the pronouns correct? 8C1a

A. She and her went to the party together.

B. We saw her and he together at the mall.

C. Dave asked John and he to help wash the dishes.

D. We and they will be going to a new school next year.

9. Which of the following is a complete simple sentence? 8C1b

A. His stories are hard to follow.

B. Mike saw the headlights, and they were very bright.

C. The mice ran; the cats were chasing them.

D. Looking for my keys but I couldn't find them.

10. Which of the following is a fragment? 8C1b

A. He likes hamburgers.

B. My school is five miles from here.

C. Joe went home.

D. By the time Casey got over there.

11. Which sentence below is written correctly? 8C1g

A. After the birthday party Chris asked? "do you like your new jacket"?

B. After the birthday party Chris asked, "Do you like your new jacket"?

C. After the birthday party Chris asked, "do you like your new jacket?"

D. After the birthday party Chris asked, "Do you like your new jacket?"

12. Which would be a good topic sentence to begin the second paragraph of the passage below? 8W1

> Around 1295, the people of Florence, Italy decided to build a great cathedral. They wanted the dome on the cathedral to be bigger than any that had ever been built, but they had no idea how to go about it. All the carpenters said a dome that size would weigh so much it would never stay up. So, they built the rest of the cathedral first. After eighty years they still had no idea how to build the dome.

A. About this time Brunelleschi was born and all through his childhood he heard architects and businessmen argue with carpenters and city politicians about how to build the dome.

B. When businessmen finally gave money to build the dome, they got serious about coming up with a plan.

C. When Brunslleschi was a young man, he began dreaming of a design of his own.

D. They finally decided to hold a contest to find a designer for the dome.

13. In the sentence below, which pronouns belong in the spaces? 8C1a

> Later that day, _____ and _____ went over to Amy's house.

A. he; her   C. she; I

B. he; me   D. she; him

14. Which words make up the adverb clause in the following sentence? 8C1f

> Wait where I can see you from the car.

A. I can see you

B. wait where I can see you

C. from the car

D. where I can see you

15. Which sentence below is punctuated correctly? 8C1e

A. "If you still want to go to Mark's house after lunch," said Mom, "I'll be ready to take you there".

B. "If you still want to go to Mark's house after lunch," said Mom, "I'll be ready to take you there."

C. "If you still want to go to Mark's house after lunch", said Mom, "I'll be ready to take you there."

D. "If you still want to go to Mark 's house after lunch" said Mom, "I'll be ready to take you there."

16. Which sentence below is a fragment?

A. I'll let you know when we get there.

B. Where did my dog go? 8C1b

C. I lost my sock.

D. After we reached our house last night.

17. In the sentence below, what change should be made to correct the capitalization error? 8C1g

> Our street used to be called Wigley road, however, it is now part of Shallowford Place.

A. Use a small letter *p* in *Place*.

B. Use a capital *S* in *Street*.

C. Use a capital *R* in *Road*.

D. Use a capital *H* in *however*.

Use the outline below to answer the question which follows.

> I. West Nile Virus
>   A. Symptoms of the disease
>   1. Symptoms in humans
>   2. Symptoms in animals
>   B. How the disease spreads
>   1. Mosquitoes
>   2. Birds
>   3. Horses
>   4. Blood donors
>   C. Treatment
>   1. Hospitalization
>   2. Antibiotics

18. Where would the additional entry "Kissing an infected person" fit in the outline above? 8W1

A. I C. 3   C. I A. 3

B. I B. 5   D. I D.

19. Where does the phrase "with the hole in it" belong in the sentence below?

8C1b   8C1b

> You need to bring in your tire to the store with the hole in it.

A. between *bring* and *in*

B. between *in* and *your*

C. between *tire* and *to*

D. after *store*

20. How would the sentence below change if *horse* were changed to *horses*?   8C1a

The horse in the show wore a hat on his head.

A. The horses in the show wore a hat on their head.

B. The horses in the show wore hats on their heads.

C. The horses in the show wore a hat on their heads.

D. The horses in the show wore a hat on his head.

21. Which word makes a transition in the paragraph below?   8W1

People in California thought waiting three weeks for their mail was just too long. A company in Missouri started the Pony Express to solve the problem. Pony Express riders would ride fast for 10 miles and then switch to a fresh horse for the next 10 miles. After 70 miles and 7 horses, the rider would rest and hand off the mailbags to a fresh rider. Finally, in just 10 days the mail arrived in San Francisco.

A. Pony Express

B. Switch

C. After

D. Finally

22. Read the sentence below. Then identify the underlined part of the sentence.

8C2f

> Although I am new here, I feel very much at home

A. adverb clause

B. prepositional phrase

C. independent clause

D. adjective clause

23. Read the four sentences. Then choose the answer that shows the BEST order for the sentences.   8W1

1. Victor went to the laundry room and began to sort clothes.

2. Before putting the clothes in the washing machine, he turned on the water and poured the detergent.

3. Then he put in his first load of clothes.

4. When Victor began to dress, he realized most of his clothes were dirty.

A. 4, 1, 2, 3   C. 1, 2, 3, 4

B. 3, 2, 1, 4   D. 2, 3, 4, 1

24. Read the sentence. Choose the transitional word or words that BEST fit the blank.   8C1b

> Desiree likes watching romantic comedies; _____, Tristan prefers action movies.

A. in other words

B. as a result

C. however

D. furthermore

25. Read the paragraph. Choose the sentence that would be the BEST concluding sentence. 8W1

Two children were playing in the street. They did not hear the approaching car until they heard the screeching of the tires. They looked up to see their mother's terrified expression.

A. They knew the sitter and they were in trouble.

B. Other children were playing in the street.

C. They were jumping rope.

D. Their mother's name was Fran.

26. Choose the sentence that would be appropriate in a friendly letter but NOT appropriate for a formal report. 8W2

A. Stephen King wrote his first short story when he was only seven years old.

B. When Mark Twain wrote *The Adventures of Huckleberry Finn*, he put the book aside for several years because he couldn't figure out what to do after Huck and Jim had floated past Cairo.

C. Although Emily Dickinson wrote over seventeen hundred poems, only seven were published during her lifetime.

D. Henry Wadsworth Longfellow wrote "The Cross of Snow" in memory of his wife, who had died in a fire.

27. Choose the sentence that contains an error. 8C1g

A. This mess was made by someone with a key to this classroom.

B. My pet dog, Harley, loves to chase imaginary cats up trees.

C. All the corections have now been made.

D. Taylor was impressed by the big slides at the park.

28. Read the definition. Then choose the sentence in which the underlined word has the meaning given in the definition. 8W2

Definition: study or group of studies

A. The burlap material was very <u>coarse</u>.

B. The customer's <u>coarse</u> language was offensive.

C. Jerome played eighteen holes of golf at the golf <u>course</u>.

D. Cindy needs one more <u>course</u> in math before she can graduate.

29. Read the four sentences. Then choose the BEST order for the sentences in a paragraph. 8W1

1. Derek stole the basketball out of Sam's hands.

2. Eric threw the basketball into the basket.

3. Sam dribbled the basketball to the other side of the court.

4. Derek passed the basketball to Eric.

A. 3, 4, 2, 1   C. 3, 1, 4, 2

B. 2, 3, 1, 4   D. 1, 3, 2, 4

30. Identify the letter above the part of the sentence that must be changed to make the sentence correct. 8C1g

      a   b

Mr. Krenshaw, / a renowned journalist, / was seated

        c   d

next to deacon Powers / at the wedding.

A. a   B. b   C. c   D. d

31. Which sentence should be removed from the paragraph below?   8W1

1. My first day in high school was pretty challenging. **2.** For the first time, I changed to a different class every fifty minutes. **3.** The school was huge, and I got lost during every move. **4.** I showed up to every class late. **5.** To top it all off, the combination to my locker didn't work, so I had to carry all of my books the entire day. **6.** I was not looking forward to going home, either, because I had to mow the lawn. **7.** My only consolation was that the other students in my classes were really friendly, and the teachers were understanding about what happens that first day.

A. Sentence 7   C. Sentence 2

B. Sentence 6   D. Sentence 1

32. Jim wants to research on his computer what fuels can be developed from oil. Which word(s) should he use as key words to find information?   8W2

A. crude oil   C. oil drilling

B. oil refining   D. jet fuel

33. What is the purpose of the sentence below?   8C1f

While someone is reading, we should listen.

A. to ask a question

B. to make a request

C. to make a statement

D. to express excitement

34. Priscilla wants to find a better word than "crazy" to describe something. Where should she look?   8W2

A. dictionary   C. encyclopedia

B. thesaurus   D. internet

Read the paragraph below, then answer questions 35 – 37 that follow.

Komodo Dragons

(1) Komodo dragons are the largest living reptiles in the world. (2) Ten feet long is how big they can grow. (3) They are good and limber climbers and fast runners, but not far. (4) These voracious eater's love to dine on deer and wild boar. (5) Even one bite is deadly, as Komodos carry poisonous bacteria in their mouths. (6) Long forked tongues help them track fallen prey. (7) Like all reptiles, though, they eat much less often than mammals of their size. (8) The largest monitor lizards, they spend their days sunning and their nights in shallow burrows. (9) Discovered on the islands of the Indonesian archipelago at the start of the 20th century, Komodos are endangered, with only a few thousand left. (10) The islands of Padar and Rinca now serve as nature reserves to protect them.

35. Which of the following is the BEST way to rewrite sentence (2)?   8C1d

A. How big they can grow is ten feet long.

B. They can grow as much as ten feet long.

C. They can grow as big as like ten feet long.

D. Leave as is.

36. Which of the following is the BEST way to rewrite sentence (3)?   8C1d

A. They are good and limber climbers, and they can run fast, but not very far.

B. They are good and limber climbers, fast runners, but nor very far.

C. They are good and limber climbers and though they can run fast, they are not distance runners.

D. Leave as is

37. Which of the following is the BEST way to rewrite sentence (8)?   8C1d

A. The largest monitor lizards, they spend their days sunning and their nights in shallow burrows.

B. The largest monitor lizards, spend their days sunning and their nights in shallow burrows.

C. The largest monitor lizards spend their days sunning and their nights in shallow burrows.

D. Leave as is

For questions 8 – 9, choose the answer that is the most effective substitute for the sentence. If no substitution is necessary, choose "Leave as is."

38. Whimpering softly was done by my new puppy all night long the first time it was away from its mother.   8C1d

A. The first time my new puppy was away from its mother, it whimpered softly all night long.

B. All night long, the first time it was away from its mother, my new puppy whimpered softly.

C. My new puppy, the first time it was away from its mother, whimpered softly all night long.

D. Leave as is.

39. A mosquito bit Mary's arm while picking up shells at the beach.   8C1d

A. While picking up shells, a mosquito bit Mary's arm at the beach.

B. Picking up shells at the beach, a mosquito bit Mary's arm.

C. While Mary was picking up shells at the beach, a mosquito bit her arm.

D. Leave as is.

40. Select the sentence fragment   8C1b

A. She flew to an island resort.

B. Repeating the same long story.

C. The horses were enjoying the day.

D. Some people didn't leave.

41. Select the underlined word in the sentence that is misspelled   8C1g

Sylvara was a beutiful acrobat who had perfect balance.

A. beutiful   C. perfect

B. acrobat   D. balance

Read the following paragraph and then answer the question that follows.

1. Everyone on both teams was completely focused on winning because the rivalry between the schools was so serious. 2. The basketball game was very intense. 3. My brother was on my team which made us even more competitive on the court. 4. Our football team made three touchdowns during the entire year. 5. The fans would remember this game as the most exciting of the season.

42. Which sentence contains an unrelated idea?   8W1

A. Sentence 1   C. Sentence 3

B. Sentence 2   D. Sentence 4

For questions 43 – 45, chose the correct word to put in the blank.

43. "Which of these two glues will dry _____?" Jeff asked the hardware store clerk.   8C1f

A. more quick   C. most quickly

B. quickly   D. more quickly

44. I _____ the winning number yesterday.   8C1d

A. drawed   C. drawn

B. drew   D. draw

45. Steve got up and followed _____ and _____.   8C1a

A. she; him   C. him; she

B. he; she   D. him; her

Select the sentence fragment in each word group.

46. A.   To finish my project.

    B.   The coastal breeze was chilly.

    C.   I did my homework.   8C1d

    D.   She went to Atlanta.

47. A.   Lorraine sighed.   8C1b

    B.   I interrupted the meeting.

    C.   Yes, right away.

    D.   We arrived too late.

Select the sentence that is rewritten correctly.

48. **Brad and his friend, Bethany, served the seven course dinner looking well-dressed to the guests.**   8C1c

    A.   Looking well-dressed to the guests, the seven course dinner served Brad and his friend, Bethany.

    B.   Brand and his friend, Bethany, served the seven course dinner to the guests looking well-dressed.

    C.   Brad and his friend, Bethany, served the well-dressed seven course dinner to the guests.

    D.   Looking well-dressed, Brad and his friend, Bethany, served the seven course dinner to the guests.

49. **The batter smiled at the fans hitting a home run on the first pitch.**   8C1c

    A.   The batter smiled at the fans which hit a home run on the first pitch.

    B.   The batter smiled at the fans who hit a home run on the first pitch.

    C.   Hitting a home run on the first pitch, the batter smiled at the fans.

    D.   Leave as is.

Chose the answer that is the most effective substitute for the underlined part of the sentence.

50. **She picked up her <u>book, the</u> cover was bent so she knew someone had been reading it**   8C1b

    A.   book: the   C.   book and the

    B.   book; the   D.   Leave as is

For questions 51 – 53, copy the following sentences adding all missing punctuation and correcting any capitalization errors.

51. **Amanda volunteers to help with the children at the women's shelter.**   8C1g

52. **mr. owens had a successful business but he always wanted to travel to south america.**   8C1e, 8C1g

53. **The teacher asked the class how many of you did your homework**   8C1e, 8C1g

For questions 54 – 56, combine the sentences into one sentence. Be sure to punctuate and capitalize correctly.

54. **David loved going to high school football games. When he got to high school he tried out for the team.**   8C1b, 8C1e

55. **I have to wash the car. I have to do the dishes. Then I have to finish my history project before I can go with you.**   8C1b, 8C1e

56. **Doug picked up his bat. He walked over to the plate. He hit his first home run.**   8C1b, 8C1e

For questions 57 – 60, copy the sentences correcting dangling modifiers, unclear pronoun references, and adverb, adjective, or verb errors.

57. **The girl was carrying her cat down the street wearing a long skirt.**   8C1c

58. **Dressed appropriate for the occasion, John went to the party.**   8C1f

59. **The pizza box was empty, but we were tired of eating it anyway.**   8C1a

60. Jessica be getting the news of the breakup from Erica.   8C1d

For questions 61 – 65, answer the question or follow the directions and write on your own paper.

61. Greg wants to find a word that means the same as "peculiar." Where should he look?   8W2

62. Write two to three words which could be used as transition word between paragraphs when ordering the information chronologically.   8W1

63. Rewrite the sentence below to ensure it reflects the 2nd person point of view consistently.   8W4

> I am riding my bike through her neighborhood in the hopes of finding out what happened to my dog.

64. Read the passage below with sentences arranged in random order and determine which organizational form the paragraph should take and why (i.e. compare/contrast, cause/effect, order of importance, and so on).   8W1

1. There is no stop sign at the intersection of McCleskey and Broad.

2. Two children were almost hit by passing vehicles while crossing the Broad Street intersection.

3. A truck hit a sports car in a slide collision at McCleskey and Broad.

4. People often exceed the speed limit while going through the intersection of McCleskey and Broad.

65. In describing how to operate a push button pen, one person wrote, "Put your thumb on the top thing and let go so you can write." Rewrite this sentence to make the direction clearer.   8W4

Index